Crave

Cupcakes, Cakes, Cookies, *and More* from an Iconic Bakery

CAROLYNE MCINTYRE JACKSON
& JODI WILLOUGHBY

To our husbands and sons, your love and belief in us have been instrumental to our success. We are where we are today because of you.

To our mom, thank you for instilling in us resilience and grit, qualities that have carried us through challenges with strength.

To our sister Antoinette, your support and presence have been a constant source of encouragement.

To our dad, though you have not been with us for a very long time, your legacy continues in our strong work ethic and entrepreneurial spirit.

To all the dedicated individuals who have been part of our Crave team, past and present, we express our heartfelt gratitude. Your contributions have shaped our vision and fuelled our passion.

To all our friends and customers who have trusted us to be a part of everyday moments and celebrations, thank you for supporting us for more than twenty years.

With all of you, we've achieved more than we ever thought possible.

Thank you.

Contents

Introduction

By the time this book goes to print, Crave will have celebrated twenty years in business. We are incredibly proud to share this collection of recipes with you. Each of these recipes has undergone thousands of hours of testing, from initial flavour concepts to being freshly baked in our bakeries each day. This cookbook guarantees delicious outcomes for everyone—from the beginner to the experienced baker—no matter the occasion. Whether you're celebrating a first birthday or a ninety-ninth, celebrating a new job, or making snacks for lunches, you can trust these recipes will turn out delicious baked treats every time.

We grew up on a farm in southern Alberta outside of High River, surrounded by a family of talented bakers, including our mom, grandmothers, and aunts. Baking from scratch was the only thing we knew (Oreos were a rare treat!), and these traditions were passed down to us over the years. As we ventured out to pursue our own paths—attending university and then entering the workforce—we continued to share our love of baking for others. Whether it was baking cookies for friends or offering to make birthday cakes for co-workers, we have always had a passion for making people happy through baking.

In 2003 we came up with the idea to start a home-based cookie business. We had a friend create our first logo and menu, then we rented a commercial kitchen and baked cookies for our cousins to give as Christmas gifts to their corporate clients. We delivered pale-blue cookie boxes across the city and received follow-up orders.

Then came decision time: should we open a bakery? We explored options, including renting a commercial kitchen or converting a home basement into a commercial kitchen to run a stall at a farmers' market outside the city. We worked on a business plan to sell cookies and cupcakes, then found a store front in Kensington. With our own savings and a small loan from the bank, we set about converting what used to be an Internet café into a bakery. At every step, we worked with friends on the design and build, carefully selecting the perfect white paint to complement our buttercream frosting colours and create an inviting store experience for the customers we hoped would walk through our door.

In September 2004, we opened the doors of Crave! With a mix of fear and confidence, we proudly baked and shared our cupcakes and cookies with the people of Calgary. Neither of us had any formal baking training, but we knew how to work hard, get along with each other, and we had a true passion for sharing great baking. We baked our beloved family recipes, and people came; we baked every day, sold out, hired some friends to help, kept baking, and kept selling out. We baked everything from scratch, cracking every egg, unwrapping one-pound bricks of butter into KitchenAid mixers, baking cupcakes and cookies, icing our cupcakes, and putting them on display for customers to purchase. In our business plan, we set a goal to hire a pastry chef in five years—but we ended up hiring her in month five, and she still works with us today! (Thank you for sticking it out with us, Cynthia.) We were baking together, sharing our baking with so many people, and doing what we set out to do: bake cupcakes and cookies that tasted delicious. Humbly, we celebrated our wins, learned from our failures, and hired bakers and retail staff who shared our passion and love of from-scratch baking to meet the demand for Crave cupcakes. We knew we wanted Crave to have more than one location, and our growth plans started to unfold.

Together with many talented, smart, and hardworking individuals, we have grown Crave to six locations—four in Calgary, one in Edmonton, and one in Saskatoon—and we continue to set our sights on Canada-wide expansion. Since 2004, everything we have created and shared has been a labour of love. We continue to perfect our craft every day through our baking, and we have the honour of being part of people's celebrations, both big and small. And now we are delighted to share our recipes with you.

We hope you enjoy baking and sharing these recipes as much as we do. Happy baking,

Carolyne & Jodi

SISTERS AND CRAVE CO-FOUNDERS

Ingredient Staples

Following are the key ingredients we keep stocked in our bakeries and personal kitchens. Stocking your baking cupboard with these items will make baking a breeze. Most of them can be found in your local grocery store, but if you cannot find an ingredient, the internet is always a good option.

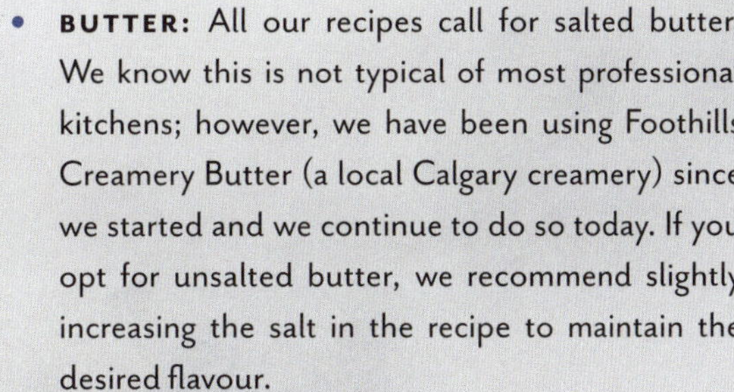

- **BUTTER:** All our recipes call for salted butter. We know this is not typical of most professional kitchens; however, we have been using Foothills Creamery Butter (a local Calgary creamery) since we started and we continue to do so today. If you opt for unsalted butter, we recommend slightly increasing the salt in the recipe to maintain the desired flavour.
- **COCOA POWDER:** All our recipes use 22–24 percent Dutch-process cocoa powder.
- **CHOCOLATE:**
    - **CHOCOLATE CHUNKS/CHIPS:** Our bakeries use Barry Callebaut chocolate chunks in dark, milk, and white. Buy the best chocolate you can find, but if you're in a pinch, Chipits chocolate chips from the grocery store will work.
    - **CHOPPED CHOCOLATE:** Our salted-chocolate-chunk recipe calls for chunks and chopped chocolate. Our bakeries use Valrhona 66 percent dark-chocolate callets. These are chopped and then added to the cookie dough. Again, use the best chocolate you can find when a recipe calls for chopped chocolate.
    - **COATING:** We use coating chocolate to dip and drizzle our cookies and cupcakes. Coating chocolate does not need to be tempered, making it easy to use for decorating.
- **CREAM CHEESE:** Always buy Philadelphia Cream Cheese in block form, not the spreadable kind.
- **DAIRY:** Typically, our recipes that require milk use 2 percent unless stated otherwise. You can substitute with 1 percent milk, but not skim milk. For whipping cream, opt for 33 or 35 percent fat content. Sour cream should have a fat content of 14 percent, though 7 percent can be used as a substitution.
- **DAIRY SUBSTITUTE:** We use oat milk in place of dairy for our vegan cupcakes, cakes, and cookies. Feel free to use whichever non-dairy substitute you prefer.

- **EGGS:** All our recipes use large-sized eggs.
- **FLOUR:** Always use unbleached all-purpose flour.
- **GLUTEN-FREE FLOUR:** We use Cup4Cup gluten-free flour.
- **GEL FOOD COLOURING:** The contentious food colouring debate. We have tried a few times to remove food colouring from our buttercream and red velvet cake, but in the end, we always go back to using our original brand, Chefmaster. Feel free to omit food colouring whenever the recipe calls for it. However, if you choose to use it, we recommend using gel food colouring, as the liquid food colouring typically found in grocery stores will not give you the same intensity of colour.
- **FRUIT AND FRUIT PURÉES:** We use fresh fruit when it is in season, then freeze any extra to use throughout the rest of the year. Our fruit-based buttercreams are crafted with real fruit purées. While this may not be readily available in grocery stores, you can substitute it by puréeing unsweetened frozen fruit.
- **OATMEAL:** Our go-to is large-flake oatmeal.
- **OIL:** Our bakeries use canola oil, but feel free to use any neutral oil you have on hand such as vegetable or safflower oil.
- **PEANUT BUTTER:** Use smooth peanut butter, not natural.
- **SPRINKLES:** In our bakeries we use all types of sprinkles. Technically, the small round-shaped sprinkles are called nonpareils, while the longer ones are referred to as jimmies. Typically, we use nonpareils for decorating and add jimmies into cake batter and cookie dough. However, sprinkles are interchangeable, so feel free to use what you have on hand or what you can purchase at the grocery store.
- **SUGARS:** One of the main ingredients in our bakeries is sugar. Recipes in this book call for granulated sugar, which is the standard white sugar found in grocery stores. For brown sugar we use golden yellow sugar, and icing sugar is just what it is—icing sugar. For decorating purposes, we use coarse sugar, which adds an extra sparkle to cookies and cupcakes.
- **UNSWEETENED APPLESAUCE:** We use this as an egg replacement in our vegan cakes and cupcakes.
- **NON-DAIRY BUTTER:** We use Becel Plant Butter. We tested several varieties of non-dairy butter, but this one worked best in the recipes.

Essential Tools

Stocking your kitchen with some of our favourite tools for baking at home will help enhance your baking experience and make it even more enjoyable. As we are a small local business, we always promote shopping locally whenever you can. The following tools can be purchased at your favourite local kitchen store, unless otherwise stated.

- **BAKING CUPS:** We always have on hand white and brown baking cups, which are essential for making cupcakes.
- **BAKING PANS:** In our bakeries we use industrial uncoated pans. However, in our home kitchens we use Williams Sonoma Goldtouch pans and USA Pan aluminized steel pans. Both brands offer non-stick options, and they can be purchased from Williams Sonoma or Amazon. Below is a recommendation of the number and sizes of pans you will need to bake the recipes in the book.
    - Two 8-inch round pans
    - Two 8-inch square pans
    - Two 12-cup cupcake tins
    - One 9- × 13-inch pan
    - Three 11- × 17-inch rimmed baking sheets
    - Two 8- × 5-inch loaf pans

- **CAKE DECORATING SUPPLIES:** For simple cake and cupcake decorating, here are some basic tools you will need.
    - **PASTRY BAGS:** Reusable 12-inch and 14-inch bags.
    - **PASTRY TIPS:** Start your collection with a 1M (large star) and 1A (large round) tip. As you get more comfortable with your piping skills, add different sized star and round tips.
    - **COUPLERS:** It's nice to have a few.
    - **OFFSET SPATULA:** A 9-inch offset spatula is an essential tool; you will find yourself wanting a few as you begin to use them.
    - **ROTATING CAKE STAND:** If you are looking to up your cake-decorating game, a rotating cake stand is essential.
    - **CAKE BOARDS:** 8-inch and 10-inch sizes.
    - A 12-inch serrated knife.
- **CANDY THERMOMETER:** Having a candy thermometer is essential for making perfect caramel.
- **COOKIE SCOOP:** Cookie scoops are essential equipment. While our bakeries have several different sizes, in our homes we typically use a size 40 (¾-ounce) or size 30 (1-ounce) handled scoop. The scoop size depends on the desired size of cookie you want to bake.
- **DIGITAL FOOD SCALE:** If there is one tool to add to your kitchen, it's a digital food scale. While all the recipes in this book provide measurements in both cups and grams, we highly recommend weighing your ingredients; it is more accurate, faster, and easier to clean up. Once you try it, we believe you won't go back! Our favourite digital scale for home kitchens is an Escali scale.
- **DIGITAL STICK THERMOMETER:** We use internal temperature readings to ensure our loaves are perfectly baked; it's a game-changing tool for taking the guesswork out of trying to determine if your loaf is fully baked or not. We recommend Thermapen digital thermometers for their ease of use, speed, and accuracy.
- **EMILE HENRY PIE PLATES:** We love all pie plates, but Emile Henry pie plates make everything in them look beautiful; they also look great on the dinner table when serving.
- **FOOD PROCESSOR:** This is an essential tool for making perfectly flaky pastry. Although a pastry blender can be used, a food processor is quicker and more efficient.
- **KITCHEN TORCH:** Absolutely not an essential tool, but s'more cookies are so much better when you toast the marshmallows!
- **MEASURING CUPS:** Although we weigh most of our ingredients, a good set of measuring cups for dry ingredients is essential. In our homes, we prefer cups with a smooth top, and we love our Pyrex glass measuring cups for liquids.
- **MEASURING SPOONS:** We use measuring spoons for smaller ingredients such as baking powder, baking soda, spices, etc.
- **PARCHMENT PAPER:** Our bakeries have always used parchment paper, but if we're being perfectly honest, we were slow to add this tool to our home kitchens. However, once you start using parchment paper, it's hard to imagine baking without it. You will find throughout the book we use both butter and parchment paper to line the baking pans. This ensures your baked goods come out of the pans easily and makes cleanup a breeze.

- **PASTRY BLENDER:** If you do not have a food processor, this is a good backup tool for making pastry.
- **PASTRY WHEEL:** This is a nice-to-have tool to cut pastry and rolled cookie dough.
- **ROLLING PIN:** This is an essential tool for rolling cookies and pastry. Our preferred rolling pin is made of wood, on the larger size (12 inches), heavy, and has handles.
- **RUBBER SPATULAS:** These are not to be confused with food turners or flippers! It's essential to have an assortment of sizes and varieties of spatulas, from spoonulas to mini spatulas; ensure you include heatproof ones in your collection.
- **RULER:** For perfectly portioned bars, our bakeries use rulers to mark the bars evenly before cutting. We do the same in our kitchens.
- **SILICONE PASTRY BRUSH:** This is essential for glazing loaves.
- **STAND MIXER:** Although not essential, if you plan on making a lot of cookies and buttercream frostings, a stand mixer will reduce your prep time significantly. In a pinch, all recipes calling for a stand mixer can be made with a hand mixer.

A Few How-Tos

Following are some basic how-tos for decorating cupcakes, cakes, and cookies. While we are not professionally trained bakers, we have spent a lot of time decorating, and we believe it's important for everyone to feel confident in both baking and decorating. We hope these how-tos will serve as a guide to make your baking journey as enjoyable as possible.

How to Fill a *Pastry* Bag

Each morning our bakeries start the day baking cupcakes and making buttercream frostings. After the cupcakes are pulled from the pans and cooled, the bakers fill pastry bags with various buttercreams to prepare the "cupcake walls" in our stores. This task is one of the most satisfying aspects of a baker's morning, as they anticipate the joy the vibrant buttercream colours will bring to customers. If you're unsure how to fill a pastry bag, follow these simple steps and you will be on your way to creating the beauty that lies in the cupcake.

To fill a pastry bag, gather the following items:

- **14-inch or 12-inch pastry bag**
- **Decorating tips**
- **Coupler**
- **Spoonula spatula**
- **Freshly prepared buttercream frosting or filling**

FOR DECORATING *cupcakes* OR *large* BORDERS ON CAKES:

- Place a 1M tip in a 14-inch pastry bag. (For large decorating tips, a coupler is not required.) Create a "C" with your hand and fold one-third of the bag over the top of your hand. Then, using a spoonula spatula, scoop buttercream into the bag until it's about half full. Pull the top of the bag up and twist it closed. Your bag is now ready to frost cupcakes, pipe borders on cakes, or whatever else your heart desires.

FOR *small*, FINE DECORATING DETAILS:

- Place a coupler inside a 12-inch pastry bag. Then place the tip onto the coupler outside the bag and secure it with the coupler screw. Proceed as above, filling the bag halfway full of buttercream frosting or filling.

How to Pipe *Buttercream* Frosting onto Cupcakes

Creating the perfect Crave swirl is one of the most important tasks in our bakeries, as the beautiful display of cupcakes greets customers as they enter the bakeries. Mastering just the right amount of buttercream frosting on top of cupcakes is a skill. Following are a few simple guidelines we use when training new team members.

- With a pastry bag half full of buttercream, hold the top of the bag in your dominant hand.
- Next, place the tip of the pastry bag in the middle of the cupcake. Apply even, steady pressure to the bag with your dominant hand as you start frosting, moving from the centre to the outside edge of the cupcake in a circular motion, gradually working your way back toward the centre. It takes three or four full turns around the cupcake to achieve the perfect swirl.

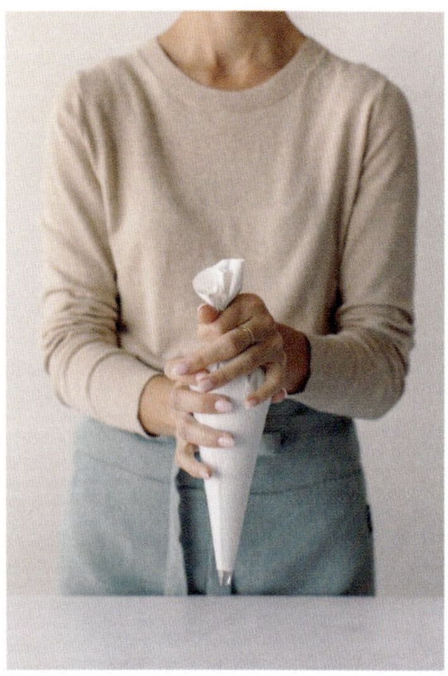

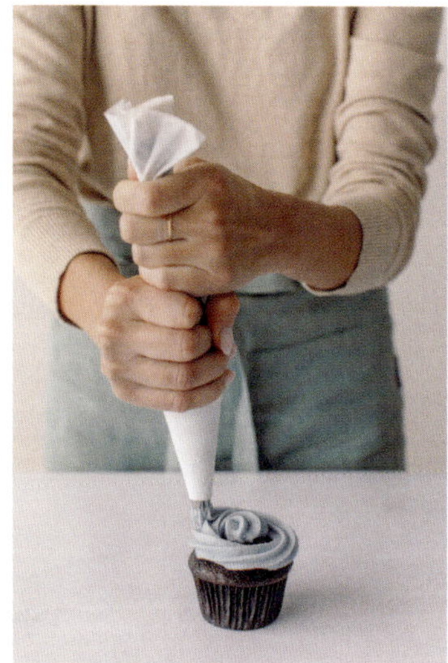

PRO TIP: The key to successful piping is controlling the pressure you apply to the pastry bag.

How to Ice a *Two*-Layer Cake

Our bakeries make gorgeous three-layer 6-inch, 8-inch and 10-inch cakes. However, we wanted to make this cookbook as approachable as possible, so we designed the recipes to make two-layer 8-inch cakes.

To start frosting your cakes, gather the following tools:

- **12-inch serrated knife**
- **10-inch cake board**
- **Offset spatula**
- **Rotating cake stand (if using)**

CUTTING THE CAKES:

- After the cakes have cooled, remove the parchment from the bottom of the cakes and trim off the domed part of the cake, removing as little cake as possible. Put the trimmed cake aside and use it as a delicious snack to share (or not) before you serve your finished cake!
- Place a small amount of buttercream in the centre of the cake board, then position one layer of cake in the middle of the board.

FILLING THE CAKE AND THE *buttercream* CRUMB COAT:

- Place approximately 1 cup (220 g) of buttercream onto the middle of the cake. Use an offset spatula to evenly spread the buttercream to the edges of the cake.
- Stack the second layer of cake, cut side down, on top of the first layer. Place approximately 1 cup (220 g) of buttercream onto the middle of the cake. Gently and evenly spread the buttercream over the sides and top of the cake. Refrigerate for 10–20 minutes.

APPLYING THE *final* COAT OF BUTTERCREAM:

- Remove the cake from the refrigerator and place approximately ¾ cup (170 g) of buttercream onto the middle of the cake. Using the offset spatula, evenly spread the buttercream over the sides and top of the cake. Repeat the process if any cake is visible through the buttercream.

How to *Add Filling* to a Layer Cake

The most common cake filling in our bakeries is buttercream. However, to create different flavour combinations, add various fillings in addition to a light layer of buttercream. Some of our favourite fillings include Vanilla or Chocolate Custard (pg 46, 48), Raspberry Jam (pg 44), and cookie crumbs.

Gather the following tools:

- **12-inch serrated knife**
- **10-inch cake board**
- **Offset spatula**
- **Rotating cake stand (if using)**

CUTTING THE CAKES:

- After the cakes have cooled, remove the parchment from the bottom of the cakes and trim off the domed part of the cake, removing as little cake as possible. Put the trimmed cake aside and use it as a delicious snack to share (or not) before you serve your finished cake!
- Place a small amount of buttercream in the centre of the cake board, then position one layer of cake in the middle of the board.

FILLING THE CAKE:

- Place approximately ½ cup (110 g) of buttercream onto the middle of the cake. Use an offset spatula to evenly spread the buttercream to the edges of the cake.
- Fill a 14-inch pastry bag (fit with a large round tip) with buttercream. Pipe a border around the outside edge of the cake to create a dam. Place ½ cup of filling or crumbs onto the middle of the cake and spread evenly with an offset spatula to the buttercream dam.
- Stack the second layer of cake, cut side down, on top of the first layer. Place approximately 1 cup (220 g) of buttercream onto the middle of the cake. Gently and evenly spread the buttercream over the sides and top of the cake. Refrigerate the cake for about 10–20 minutes.

APPLYING THE *final* COAT OF BUTTERCREAM:

- Remove the cake from the refrigerator and place approximately ¾ cup (170 g) of buttercream onto the middle of the cake. Using the offset spatula, evenly spread the buttercream over the sides and top of the cake. Repeat the process if any cake is visible through the buttercream.

How to Pipe Buttercream *Details* onto Cakes

Following are some buttercream piping guidelines for a few of our favourite cake styles. Please note a rotating cake stand is highly recommended for this section.

SHELL BORDER:

- This border style is featured on the classic cakes in our bakeries. The shell border is piped on both the bottom and top of the cake.
- Place a 1M tip inside a 14-inch pastry bag and fill about half full with buttercream frosting. Hold the bag at a forty-five-degree angle to the surface. Apply steady, even pressure and squeeze buttercream out of the tip and gently pull back while releasing the pressure to create a teardrop shape. Repeat this process, slightly overlapping the tail of each shell.

DOLLOP BORDER:

- This style is found on the Confetti Cake (pg 85), and Gluten-Free Red Velvet Cake (pg 209).
- Place a 1M (star) or 1A (round) tip inside a 14-inch pastry bag and fill about half full with buttercream frosting. Hold the bag at a ninety-degree angle to the surface. Apply steady, even pressure and squeeze buttercream out of the tip until the desired round size is achieved. Then release pressure, and pull the bag straight up and away.

HORIZONTAL RIBBED STYLE:

- This style is found on the Strawberry Cake with Strawberry Cream Cheese Buttercream Frosting (pg 95).
- Place a 1M (star) tip inside a 14" pastry bag and fill about half full with buttercream frosting. Hold the bag at a ninety-degree angle to the side of the cake. Start at the bottom of the cake, apply pressure to the bag releasing buttercream and simultaneously turn the cake stand. Stop where you started, then begin the next row of buttercream from the same starting point, slightly overlapping the first line of buttercream. Continue this process until the entire cake is covered in rows of buttercream.

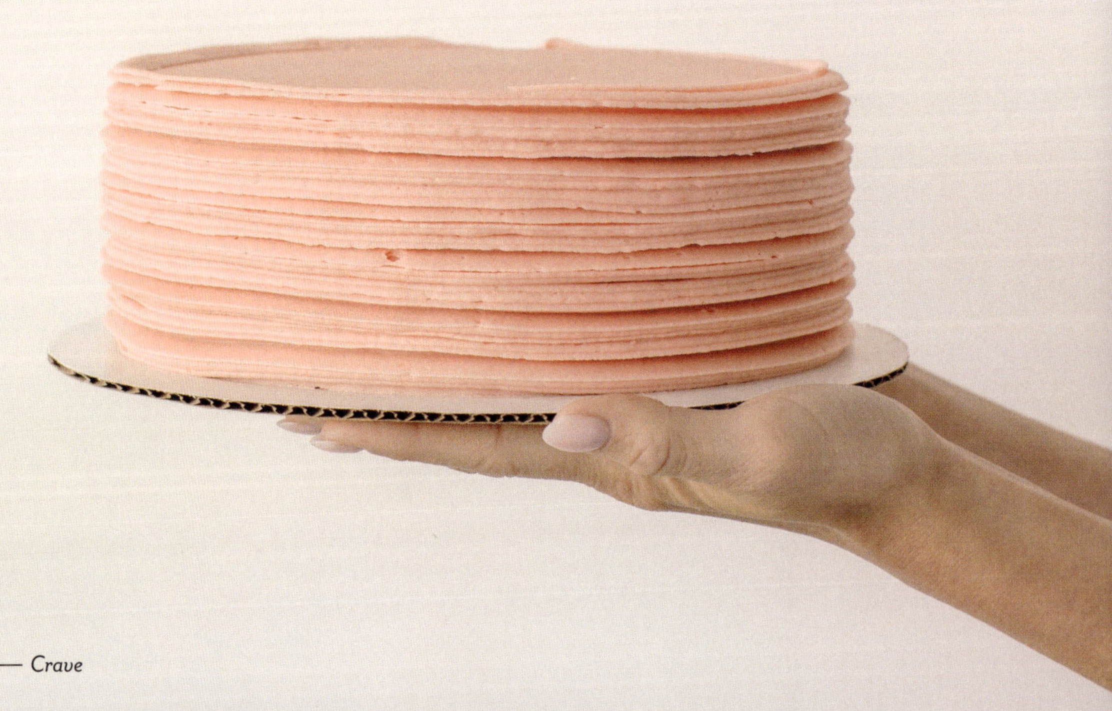

RIBBED STYLE:

- Immediately after the final coat of buttercream is applied, place an offset spatula on the side of the cake. Slowly turn the cake stand while moving the offset spatula toward the top of the cake.

SPRINKLED SIDES:

- If you wish to cover your cake sides with sprinkles, coconut, or mini chocolate chips, use the following technique immediately after the final coat of buttercream is applied.
- Fill a bowl with the ingredient you are using to cover the sides. Hold the cake flat in your hand over top of the bowl and lightly press sprinkles onto the sides of the cake. Repeat this process until the desired look is achieved.

How to *Fill* a Cupcake with Filling or Buttercream

Occasionally, one of our "Craving of the Month" flavours involves piping a filling into the middle of the cupcake, like our delicious Banana Caramel Cupcakes with Browned Butter Buttercream Frosting (pg 99).

To pipe filling into a cupcake, gather the following items:

- **Apple corer or small round cookie cutter**
- **12-inch pastry bag**
- **#10 round tip (optional)**
- **Filling for the cupcake**

TO FILL THE CUPCAKES:

- Position the apple corer or small round cookie cutter in the centre of the cupcake. Press about three-quarters of the way into the cupcake and remove the piece of cupcake.
- Transfer the filling you are using into the pastry bag, fit with a #10 round tip (if using). Pipe the filling into the hole of the cupcake until it reaches the top.
- Fill all the cupcakes, then frost with the buttercream frosting of your choice.

How to *Dip* and *Drizzle* Cookies

At Crave, our team members have a love for baking and decorating cupcakes and cakes. A few years ago we added dips and drizzles onto some of our cookies. While it's not essential for everyday cookies, if you are hosting an event and want to have your guests swooning (or thinking you bought them at your local Crave), use the following guide.

Gather the following items to drip and/or drizzle your cookies:

- **1 cup (250 g) milk or dark coating chocolate**
- **Saucepan and bowl or a microwavable bowl**
- **Parchment paper**
- **Cookie sheet**
- **12-inch pastry bag**
- **Small round tip (#3 or #4)**

Melting THE CHOCOLATE:

- The key to decorating with chocolate is using coating chocolate. If you're skilled in tempering chocolate, you can use high-quality chocolate, but for simple decorations, coating chocolate is perfect. To begin, melt the coating chocolate in a bowl set on top of a saucepan of boiling water or in a glass bowl in the microwave.

FOR HALF-DIPPING:

- Line a cookie sheet with parchment paper. Dip the cookie halfway into the melted chocolate and place it on the prepared sheet. Gently push the cookie from the non-dipped side along the parchment paper a couple of inches. This will help maintain a round edge and prevent excess chocolate from pooling on the cookie's side. If using sprinkles, sprinkle immediately after dipping to ensure they stick to the chocolate before it sets. Allow the chocolate to set before serving or storing the cookies.

FOR DRIZZLING:

- Line a cookie sheet with parchment paper and arrange your cookies close together so there is very little white space showing on the pan. Prepare a 12-inch pastry bag with a small round tip (optional) and fill it with the melted chocolate. Place your finger on the tip of the bag to prevent the chocolate from dripping out of the bag. Work quickly to drizzle all the cookies on the sheet, following a zigzag pattern. Allow the chocolate to set before serving or storing the cookies.

A Homemade Pantry

This chapter is filled with what we affectionately refer to as our homemade pantry essentials. As we were growing up on our family farm, our mom made most things we ate from scratch. We brought this principle with us when we started Crave—ensuring almost all of the ingredients we incorporate into our recipes have been carefully made from scratch. The following "pantry essential" recipes are not only integral to numerous recipes throughout the book, but they can also stand as delicious creations on their own. However, if time constraints prevent you from making something from scratch, don't hesitate to buy the store-bought version.

Graham Cracker Crumbs

Makes: About 4 cups of coarse crumbs or 2 cups of fine-ground crumbs | Prep Time: 20 minutes
Bake Time: 25–30 minutes | Cooling Time: 10–20 minutes

Once you make homemade graham crackers and crumbs at home, the store-bought varieties will pale in comparison. They are easy to make, and as they bake, your kitchen will smell delicious. Adding this recipe to your collection is a decision you'll be glad to have made.

USED IN:

Strawberry Cake with Strawberry Cream Cheese Buttercream Frosting (pg 95)
S'more Cookies (pg 127)
Coconut Cream Pie (pg 185).

INGREDIENTS:

- **1½ cups (225 g) all-purpose flour**
- **⅓ cup (50 g) whole wheat flour**
- **½ tsp salt**
- **¾ cup (170 g) butter**
- **½ cup (100 g) brown sugar**
- **2 Tbsp (40 g) light corn syrup**

1. Position a rack in the centre of your oven and preheat it to 350°F. Line a cookie sheet with parchment paper.
2. In a medium-sized bowl, add the flour, whole wheat flour, and salt. Whisk to combine and set aside.
3. In the bowl of a stand mixer fitted with a paddle attachment, beat the butter on medium speed for about a minute. Gradually add the brown sugar and corn syrup. Stop the mixer and scrape down the sides of the bowl with a spatula. Continue mixing for 5–8 minutes or until the mixture becomes pale and fluffy.
4. Stop the mixer, scrape the bowl again, then turn the mixer to low speed and gradually add the flour mixture. Continue mixing on low until a dough forms.
5. Remove the bowl from the mixer and crumble the dough evenly onto your prepared sheet.
6. Bake the crumbs for 10 minutes. Use a spatula to toss and break up the crumbs, then continue baking for another 5 minutes. Repeat the process, baking in 5-minute intervals, until the crumbs are golden brown.
7. Set the pan on a wire rack and allow the crumbs to cool completely.
8. If making fine crumbs, place all the cookie crumbs into a food processor and pulse until a fine crumb forms.
9. Store the graham crumbs in an airtight container at room temperature for up to 5 days or in the freezer for up to 3 months.

>>

Variations

GRAHAM CRACKERS (OR COOKIES IF YOU PREFER!): If you're looking to elevate your s'more game, whip up a batch of these crackers/cookies prior to heading out to the campsite!

Follow the instructions until the end of step 4. Then lightly flour your work surface, and using a rolling pin, roll the dough to ⅛-inch thickness. Cut the dough into squares using a knife or pastry wheel and place them 2 inches apart on a parchment-lined cookie sheet. Bake at 350°F for 8–10 minutes or until the cookies are golden brown. Allow the cookies to cool on the baking sheet for 5 minutes before transferring them to a wire rack to cool completely.

Chocolate Cookie Crumbs

Makes: About 4 cups | Prep Time: 20–30 minutes | Bake Time: 15–20 minutes | Cooling Time: 10–20 minutes

Just like graham crumbs, once you've made homemade chocolate cookie crumbs, there's no turning back to store-bought varieties. Use these crumbs in any recipe that calls for chocolate crumbs.

USED IN:

Cookies and Cream Buttercream Frosting (pg 67)

INGREDIENTS:

- **1¾ cups (260 g) all-purpose flour**
- **½ cup (60 g) cocoa powder, sifted**
- **Pinch salt**
- **1 cup (225 g) butter**
- **½ cup (100 g) granulated sugar**
- **2 Tbsp (25 g) brown sugar**
- **¼ cup (80 g) light corn syrup**

1. Position a rack in the centre of your oven and preheat it to 350°F. Line a cookie sheet with parchment paper.
2. In a medium-sized bowl, add the flour, cocoa powder, and salt. Whisk to combine and set aside.
3. In the bowl of a stand mixer fitted with a paddle attachment, beat the butter on medium speed for about a minute. Gradually add the sugars. Stop the mixer and use a spatula to scrape the sides of the bowl. Add the corn syrup and continue mixing on medium speed for 5–8 minutes or until the mixture becomes pale and fluffy.
4. Stop the mixer, scrape down the sides of the bowl, then turn the mixer to low speed and gradually add the flour mixture. Continue mixing on low until a dough forms.
5. Remove the bowl from the mixer and crumble the dough evenly onto your prepared sheet.
6. Bake the crumbs for 10 minutes. Use a spatula to toss and break up the crumbs, then continue baking for another 5 minutes. Repeat the process, baking in 5-minute intervals, until they are no longer shiny.
7. Set the pan on a wire rack and allow the crumbs to cool completely. Then pulse in a food processor until a fine crumb forms.
8. If making fine crumbs, place all the cookie crumbs into a food processor and pulse until a fine crumb forms.
9. Store the chocolate crumbs in an airtight container at room temperature for up to 5 days or in the freezer for up to 3 months.

Brown Sugar Crumb Topping

Makes: About 2 cups | Prep Time: 20 minutes

This is one of our most versatile recipes, with endless possibilities for use. Whether you're topping pies or loaves or making a quick fruit crisp with fruit you have on hand, this recipe will become your go-to.

USED IN:

Raspberry Sour Cream Pie (pg 175)
Raspberry Crumb Loaf (pg 199)

INGREDIENTS:

- **¾ cup (115 g) all-purpose flour**
- **½ cup (113 g) butter, softened**
- **½ cup (100 g) brown sugar**

1. Place all the ingredients in a medium-sized bowl.
2. Using your hands or a pastry blender, mix the ingredients until they are well combined and large crumbs form (the mixture should form a ball when squeezed in your hands).
3. Use the mixture as directed in the recipe.
4. Place any leftover crumb topping in an airtight container and store in the fridge for up to 5 days or in the freezer for up to 3 months.

BONUS MINI RECIPE: To make a fruit crisp, prepare 4–6 cups of sliced or chopped fruit and place in a medium-sized baking dish. If using tart fruit like rhubarb, sprinkle with 2–4 Tbsp of granulated sugar. If you're craving a bit of spice, feel free to add 1–2 tsp of your favourite spices. Top the fruit with the brown sugar crumb. Bake the crisp at 350°F for 35–45 minutes or until the fruit is soft and the crumb turns golden brown.

Farmer's Butter Glaze

Makes: About ¾ cup | Prep Time: 10 minutes | Cooling Time: 10–20 minutes

We use this glaze to top loaves and cookies. You will find several recipes in the book requiring this glaze. It sets up beautifully and make everything just a little more indulgent.

USED IN:

Auntie Louise's Gingerbread Cookies (pg 133)
Marble Loaf (pg 197)
Zucchini Pecan Loaf (pg 201)

INGREDIENTS:

- **½ cup (100 g) granulated sugar**
- **1 tsp cornstarch**
- **¼ cup (55 g) butter**
- **¼ cup (60 g) whipping cream**
- **½ tsp vanilla extract**

1. In a medium-sized saucepan, add the sugar and cornstarch and whisk to combine.
2. Add the butter and whipping cream to the saucepan and place it on the stovetop on medium heat.
3. Stir the mixture using a heatproof spatula until all the butter has melted and the mixture just begins to boil.
4. Remove the saucepan from the heat and add the vanilla.
5. Transfer the sauce to a medium-sized bowl and allow to cool for 10–20 minutes before using as directed in the recipe.
6. Store any leftover sauce in an airtight container in the fridge for up to 5 days or in the freezer for up to 3 months.

Toffee Sauce

Makes: About ¾ cup | Prep Time: 10 minutes | Bake Time: 5 minutes | Cooling Time: 10–20 minutes

This delicious, versatile toffee sauce can be used as a topping for ice cream, a sauce for cakes, or how we use it in the bakeries—mixed into buttercream to make our delicious Toffee Pecan Buttercream Frosting.

USED IN:

Toffee Pecan Buttercream Frosting (pg 69)

INGREDIENTS:

- **½ cup (120 g) whipping cream**
- **¼ cup (55 g) butter**
- **¼ cup (50 g) brown sugar**
- **2 Tbsp (40 g) golden corn syrup**
- **¼ tsp salt**
- **2 tsp vanilla extract**

1. Place the first 5 ingredients in a medium-sized saucepan and set on the stovetop on medium-high heat.
2. Stir the mixture, using a heatproof spatula, until it comes to a slow rolling boil. Boil for 3 minutes or until the sauce has thickened slightly.
3. Remove the saucepan from the heat and add the vanilla.
4. Transfer the sauce to a medium-sized bowl and allow it to cool before using as directed in the recipe.
5. Store any leftover sauce in an airtight container in the fridge for up to 5 days or in the freezer for up to 3 months.

Ganache is a staple in our bakeries. With its velvety texture and rich flavour, it's incredibly versatile. Use ganache as a topping for bars or brownies, a filling for cakes, or drizzle it over cupcakes and cookies for a finishing touch. Using corn syrup is optional, but it adds a nice sheen to the ganache.

Milk Chocolate Ganache

Makes: About ¾ cup | Prep Time: 10 minutes | Cooling Time: 10–20 minutes

USED IN:

Vanilla Thumbprint Cookies with Milk Chocolate Ganache (or Raspberry Jam) (pg 139)
Twix Bar (pg 145)

INGREDIENTS:

- **1 cup (200 g) good-quality milk chocolate chunks or chips**
- **½ cup (120 g) whipping cream**
- **1 Tbsp (20 g) light corn syrup (optional)**

1. Place the chocolate into a medium-sized bowl and set aside.
2. Place the whipping cream and corn syrup (if using) in a medium-sized saucepan and set on the stovetop on medium-high heat.
3. Bring the cream just to a boil, then immediately pour it over the chocolate. Allow it to stand for 30 seconds. Using a spatula, vigorously mix until all the chocolate has melted and the mixture is smooth.
4. Use the ganache as directed in the recipe.
5. Place any leftover ganache in an airtight container and store in the fridge for up to 5 days or in the freezer for up to 3 months.

Dark Chocolate Ganache

Makes: About 1 cup | Prep Time: 10 minutes | Cooling Time: 10–20 minutes

USED IN:

Triple Chocolate Brownie (pg 149)

INGREDIENTS:

- **⅔ cup (125 g) good quality dark chocolate chunks**
- **⅔ cup (120 g) whipping cream**
- **1 Tbsp (20 g) light corn syrup (optional)**

1. Place the chocolate into a medium-sized bowl and set aside.
2. Place the whipping cream and corn syrup (if using) in a medium-sized saucepan and set on the stovetop on medium-high heat.
3. Bring the cream just to a boil, then immediately pour it over the chocolate. Allow it to stand for 30 seconds. Using a spatula, vigorously mix until all the chocolate has melted and the mixture is smooth.
4. Use the ganache as directed in the recipe.
5. Place any leftover ganache in an airtight container and store in the fridge for up to 5 days or in the freezer for up to 3 months.

Raspberry Jam

Makes: About 1 cup | Prep Time: 10–15 minutes | Cooling Time: 10–20 minutes

This quick refrigerator jam is perfect as a filling for cakes, sandwiching between cookies, or topping thumbprint cookies. It's easy to make and can be stored in the refrigerator for up to a month.

USED IN:

Vanilla Thumbprint Cookies with Milk Chocolate Ganache (or Raspberry Jam) (pg 139)

INGREDIENTS:

- **1½ cups (300 g) granulated sugar**
- **1 cup (280 g) raspberries, frozen or fresh**
- **2 Tbsp (30 g) pectin**

1. Place all the ingredients into a large-sized saucepan and bring to rolling boil over medium-high heat, stirring occasionally with a wooden spoon. Boil for 5 minutes, then remove from the heat.
2. If you prefer fewer seeds in your jam, set a mesh strainer over a bowl and strain ⅔ to ¾ of the jam. Then add the strained jam to the seeded jam and mix thoroughly. If you like seeds in your jam, skip this step!
3. Use the jam as directed in the recipe.
4. Place any leftover jam in an airtight container and store in the fridge for up to a month.

The following are classic custard recipes that are incredibly versatile and can be used for cream pie fillings, cake or cupcake fillings, or on their own topped with fresh berries and whipped cream.

Vanilla Custard

Makes: About 3 cups | Prep Time: 10 minutes | Cooling Time: 10–20 minutes

INGREDIENTS:

- **½ cup (100 g) granulated sugar**
- **3 Tbsp (30 g) cornstarch**
- **Pinch salt**
- **2 egg yolks**
- **2½ cups (620 g) milk**
- **1 tsp vanilla extract**

1. In a medium-sized saucepan, whisk together the sugar, cornstarch, and salt. Add the egg yolks and whisk until a smooth paste forms. Then pour in the milk, whisking until fully combined.
2. Place the saucepan on the stovetop over medium-high heat and stir continuously until the mixture comes to a boil. Boil for 30 seconds or until it thickens to a custard-like consistency.
3. Remove the saucepan from the heat and stir in the vanilla.
4. Transfer the custard to a bowl (or use as directed in the recipe) and cover the surface directly with a piece of plastic wrap to prevent a skin from forming.
5. Place any leftover custard in an airtight container and store in the fridge for up to 5 days.

Coconut Custard

Makes: About 3 cups | Prep Time: 10 minutes | Cooling Time: 10–20 minutes

USED IN:

Coconut Cream Pie (pg 185)

INGREDIENTS:

- **½ cup (100 g) granulated sugar**
- **3 Tbsp (30 g) cornstarch**
- **Pinch salt**
- **2 egg yolks**
- **One 13.5-ounce (400-ml) can coconut milk**
- **½ cup (125 g) milk**

1. In a medium-sized saucepan, whisk together the sugar, cornstarch, and salt. Add the egg yolks and whisk until a smooth paste forms. Then pour in the coconut milk and the milk, whisking until fully combined.
2. Place the saucepan on the stovetop over medium-high heat and stir continuously until the mixture comes to a boil. Boil for 30 seconds or until it thickens to a custard-like consistency.
3. Remove the saucepan from the heat.
4. Transfer the custard to a bowl (or use as directed in the recipe) and cover the surface directly with a piece of plastic wrap to prevent a skin from forming.
5. Place any leftover custard in an airtight container and store in the fridge for up to 5 days.

Chocolate Custard

Makes: About 3 cups | Prep Time: 10 minutes | Cooling Time: 10–20 minutes

USED IN:

Chocolate Banana Cream Pie (pg 183)

INGREDIENTS:

- **½ cup (100 g) granulated sugar**
- **3 Tbsp (25 g) cocoa powder, sifted**
- **3 Tbsp (30 g) cornstarch**
- **Pinch salt**
- **2 egg yolks**
- **2½ cups (620 g) milk**
- **1 tsp vanilla extract**

1. In a medium-sized saucepan, whisk together the sugar, cocoa powder, cornstarch, and salt. Add the egg yolks and whisk until a smooth paste forms. Then pour in the milk, whisking until fully combined.
2. Place the saucepan on the stovetop over medium-high heat and stir continuously until the mixture comes to a boil. Boil for 30 seconds or until it thickens to a custard-like consistency.
3. Remove the saucepan from the heat and stir in the vanilla.
4. Transfer the custard to a bowl (or use as directed in the recipe) and cover the surface directly with a piece of plastic wrap to prevent a skin from forming.
5. Place any leftover custard in an airtight container and store in the fridge for up to 5 days.

Browned Butter

Makes: Slightly under 1 cup | Prep Time: 5–10 minutes | Cooling Time: 10–20 minutes

Browned butter is simple to make and adds a wonderful caramelly-nutty flavour to your baked goods. Keep in mind, though, browned butter is not always interchangeable with regular butter due to the reduced water content that results from the browning process. The recipes in this book have been adjusted to account for this.

USED IN:

Browned Butter Buttercream Frosting (pg 63)

INGREDIENTS:

- **½ pound (225 g) cubed butter**

1 To brown the butter, place the butter into a medium-sized saucepan over medium heat. Once the butter is melted, continue heating. It will foam and rise quite a bit in the pan, but once the foam subsides, stir constantly until the milk solids turn a deep golden brown. Be vigilant, as this process can happen quite quickly.

2 Transfer the melted butter and all the solids into a bowl and allow it to cool. If not using right away, place in an airtight container and store in the fridge for up to 5 days.

Caramel Filling

Makes: About 1½ cups | Prep Time: 20–30 minutes | Cooling Time: 10–20 minutes

Making caramel is not for the faint of heart. Caramel can go from perfect to burnt in seconds. Learning to make homemade caramel takes practice and patience, but once you have mastered it, you will find yourself making it more often, even for a weeknight treat. This recipe is intended for use as a filling for cakes.

USED IN:

Banana Caramel Cupcakes with Browned Butter Buttercream Frosting (pg 99)

INGREDIENTS:

- **¾ cup (150 g) whipping cream**
- **½ tsp vanilla extract**
- **⅓ cup (80 g) water**
- **1½ cups (300 g) granulated sugar**
- **2 Tbsp (40 g) light corn syrup**
- **½ tsp salt**
- **1 tsp lemon juice**
- **⅓ cup (75 g) butter, cubed**

1. Place the whipping cream and the vanilla into a small-sized saucepan and bring to a boil over medium heat. (This step can also be done in a microwave using a microwave-safe bowl.) Cover and set aside until needed.
2. Add the water, sugar, corn syrup, and salt into a medium-sized pot. Combine with a spatula, then cover with a plate and bring to a boil over medium-high heat.
3. Continue to boil the sugar mixture, swirling the pan occasionally until the mixture turns a golden amber colour.
4. Remove the pot from the heat and carefully pour the warm cream into the hot sugar, whisking constantly until combined. *Be sure to wear an oven mitt on your stirring hand, as there can be lots of steam, and the caramel will bubble and splatter.*
5. Add the lemon juice and whisk until combined. Then add the butter and whisk until the mixture is well combined.
6. Transfer the caramel to a medium-sized bowl and use as directed in the recipe.
7. Place any leftover caramel in an airtight container and store in the fridge for up to 3 weeks.

Caramel Sauce

Makes: About 1 cup / Prep Time: 20–30 minutes / Cooling Time: 10–20 minutes

This sauce is for drizzling! Use as a topping on your favourite desserts or drizzled on top of buttercream frosted cupcakes and cakes. You can also mix it into your buttercream.

USED IN:

Caramel Buttercream Frosting (pg 68)

INGREDIENTS:

- **½ cup (120 g) whipping cream**
- **1 tsp vanilla extract**
- **2 Tbsp (30 g) water**
- **¾ cup (150 g) granulated sugar**
- **1½ Tbsp (30 g) light corn syrup**
- **2 Tbsp (30 g) butter**
- **½ tsp salt**

1. Place the whipping cream and vanilla into a small-sized saucepan and bring to a boil over medium heat. (This step can also be done in a microwave using a microwave-safe bowl.) Cover and set aside until needed.
2. Add the water, sugar, and corn syrup into a medium-sized pot. Combine with a spatula, then cover with a plate and bring to a boil over medium-high heat.
3. Continue to boil the sugar mixture, swirling the pan occasionally until the mixture turns a golden amber colour.
4. Remove the pot from the heat and carefully pour the warm cream into the hot sugar, whisking constantly until combined. *Be sure to wear an oven mitt on your stirring hand, as there can be lots of steam, and the caramel will bubble and spatter.*
5. Add the butter and salt and whisk until well combined.
6. Transfer the caramel to a medium-sized bowl and use as directed in the recipe.
7. Place any leftover caramel in an airtight container and store in the fridge for up 3 weeks.

Crave's Famous Buttercream Frostings

On the following pages, you'll find our collection of never-before-published buttercream frosting recipes. Our buttercream frosting has been likened to our "superpower," with some speculating about a secret ingredient that makes it so delicious. Well, the truth is, there is no secret ingredient—rather, simple ones combined with a little love. Buttercream frosting is incredibly flexible; you can adjust the amount of icing sugar, add colour, omit colour, incorporate different extracts, to make it your own. So go ahead—have fun and experiment with the recipes to create your own perfect buttercream frosting.

Vanilla Buttercream Frosting

Makes: About 3½ cups | Prep Time: 15–20 minutes

This recipe serves as the foundation for many of our beloved buttercream frostings.

INGREDIENTS:

- **4¼ cups (560 g) icing sugar**
- **½ cup (120 g) whipping cream**
- **1¼ cups (280 g) butter, softened**
- **2 tsp vanilla extract**

1 Measure the icing sugar into a large bowl and set aside.

2 Measure the whipping cream into a glass measuring cup or small bowl and set aside.

3 In the bowl of a stand mixer fitted with a paddle attachment, beat the butter on medium speed for 2–3 minutes.

4 Stop the mixer and scrape down the sides of the bowl. With the mixer on low speed, gradually add the icing sugar, then slowly add the whipping cream and vanilla. Continue to mix on low for about a minute or until it is well combined.

5 Stop the mixer, scrape down the sides of the bowl, then turn the mixer to medium-high speed and beat for 5 minutes. Turn off the mixer, scrape down the sides of the bowl again, and add any desired food colouring. Resume mixing at medium-high speed for an additional 5–10 minutes or until the frosting is light and fluffy to the touch.

6 Use buttercream frosting as directed in the recipe.

7 Place any leftover buttercream frosting in an airtight container and store in the fridge for up to 5 days or in the freezer for up to 3 months.

NOTE: To determine when your buttercream frosting is ready, scoop a small amount onto your spatula, then gently tap it against the side of the bowl. If the buttercream frosting easily falls off the spatula, it is ready. If it stays on the spatula, continue mixing on medium-high speed until it reaches the desired consistency.

>>

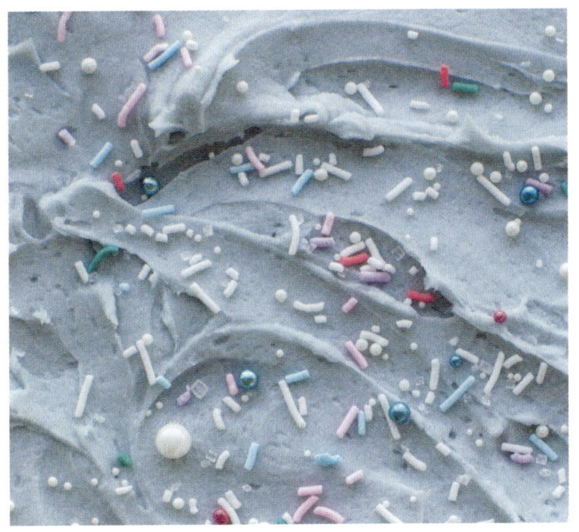

Variations

CRAVE-O-LICIOUS BUTTERCREAM FROSTING: Add 3 drops of violet and 2 drops of royal blue gel food colouring.

VAVA VANILLA BUTTERCREAM FROSTING: Add 3 drops of rose-pink gel food colouring.

MINT BUTTERCREAM FROSTING: Substitute peppermint extract for vanilla extract. Use 3 drops of leaf green gel food colouring.

Lemon Buttercream Frosting

Makes: About 3½ cups | Prep Time: 15–20 minutes

When we first opened Crave, one of our original cupcake flavours was lemon-lime, featuring lemon cake with a lime buttercream frosting. However, it always seemed to be the one left over at the end of the day, so we replaced it with what is now known as our Lemon Drop Cupcake—lemon buttercream frosting on top of a vanilla cupcake.

INGREDIENTS:

- **4½ cups (560 g) icing sugar**
- **⅓ cup (70 g) whipping cream**
- **⅓ cup (80 g) lemon juice**
- **1¼ cups (280 g) butter, softened**
- **¼ tsp lemon extract**
- **¼ tsp vanilla extract**
- **1 drop golden yellow gel food colouring**

1. Measure the icing sugar into a large bowl and set aside.
2. Measure the whipping cream and lemon juice into two separate glass measuring cups or small bowls and set aside.
3. In the bowl of a stand mixer fitted with a paddle attachment, beat the butter on medium speed for 2–3 minutes.
4. Stop the mixer and scrape down the sides of the bowl. With the mixer on low speed, gradually add the icing sugar, then slowly add the whipping cream, lemon juice, and extracts. Continue to mix on low for about a minute or until it is well combined.
5. Stop the mixer, scrape down the sides of the bowl, then turn the mixer to medium-high speed and beat for 5 minutes. Turn off the mixer, scrape down the sides of the bowl again, and add any desired food colouring. Resume mixing at medium-high speed for an additional 5–10 minutes or until it is light and fluffy to the touch.
6. Use buttercream frosting as directed in the recipe.
7. Place any leftover buttercream frosting in an airtight container and store in the fridge for up to 5 days or in the freezer for up to 3 months.

NOTE: To determine when your buttercream frosting is ready, scoop a small amount onto your spatula, then gently tap it against the side of the bowl. If the buttercream frosting easily falls off the spatula, it is ready. If it stays on the spatula, continue mixing on medium-high speed until it reaches the desired consistency.

Chocolate Buttercream Frosting

Makes: About 3½ cups | Prep Time: 15–20 minutes

You can find this buttercream frosting on our Just Chocolate and Dirty Blonde cupcakes. It can also be sandwiched between chocolate cookies for a take on a very famous fudgy cookie!

INGREDIENTS:

- **4¼ cups (560 g) icing sugar**
- **½ cup (60 g) cocoa powder, sifted**
- **½ cup (120 g) whipping cream**
- **2 tsp vanilla extract**
- **1¼ cups (280 g) butter, softened**

1. Measure the icing sugar into a large bowl and cocoa powder into a separate small bowl and set aside.
2. Measure the whipping cream and vanilla into a glass measuring cup and set aside.
3. In the bowl of a stand mixer fitted with a paddle attachment, beat the butter on medium speed for 2–3 minutes.
4. Stop the mixer and scrape down the sides of the bowl. With the mixer on low speed, gradually add the icing sugar, then slowly add the whipping cream and vanilla. Continue to mix on low for about a minute. Then gradually add the cocoa powder and mix for another minute or until it is well combined.
5. Stop the mixer, scrape down the sides of the bowl, then turn the mixer to medium-high speed and beat for 5 minutes. Turn off the mixer, scrape down the sides of the bowl again, then resume mixing at medium-high speed for an additional 5–10 minutes or until the buttercream is light and fluffy to the touch.
6. Use buttercream frosting as directed in the recipe.
7. Place any leftover buttercream frosting in an airtight container and store in the fridge for up to 5 days or in the freezer for up to 3 months.

NOTE: To determine when your buttercream frosting is ready, scoop a small amount onto your spatula, then gently tap it against the side of the bowl. If the buttercream frosting easily falls off the spatula, it is ready. If it stays on the spatula, continue mixing on medium-high speed until it reaches the desired consistency.

Strawberry Buttercream Frosting

Makes: About 3½ cups | Prep Time: 15–20 minutes

Strawberry Buttercream Frosting, as a topping on both chocolate and vanilla cupcakes, is a signature menu item in our bakeries.

INGREDIENTS:

- **4 cups (500 g) icing sugar**
- **⅓ cup (75 g) strawberry purée**
- **1 Tbsp whipping cream**
- **1 drop red gel food colouring**
- **1 drop burgundy gel food colouring**
- **1¼ cups (280 g) butter, softened**

1. Measure the icing sugar into a large bowl and set aside.
2. Measure the strawberry purée, whipping cream, and food colouring into a glass measuring cup or small bowl and set aside.
3. In the bowl of a stand mixer fitted with a paddle attachment, beat the butter on medium speed for 2–3 minutes.
4. Stop the mixer and scrape down the sides of the bowl. With the mixer on low speed, gradually add the icing sugar, then slowly add the strawberry purée mixture. Continue to mix on low for about a minute or until it is well combined.
5. Stop the mixer, scrape down the sides of the bowl, then turn the mixer to medium-high speed and beat for 5 minutes. Turn off the mixer, scrape down the sides of the bowl again, then resume mixing at medium-high speed for an additional 5–10 minutes or until the buttercream is light and fluffy to the touch.
6. Use buttercream frosting as directed in the recipe.
7. Place any leftover buttercream frosting in an airtight container and store in the fridge for up to 5 days or in the freezer for up to 3 months.

NOTE: To determine when your buttercream frosting is ready, scoop a small amount onto your spatula, then gently tap it against the side of the bowl. If the buttercream frosting easily falls off the spatula, it is ready. If it stays on the spatula, continue mixing on medium-high speed until it reaches the desired consistency.

Cream Cheese Buttercream Frosting

Makes: About 3½ cups | Prep Time: 15–20 minutes

Our Red Velvet Cupcake (pg 83) owes its fame to this buttercream frosting. In addition to our red velvet cupcakes, we pair it with chocolate to make our our Dark Angel cupcake and sandwich it between dark chocolate cookies for our take on a famous chocolate sandwich cookie!

INGREDIENTS:

- **4¼ cups (560 g) icing sugar**
- **1¼ cups (280 g) butter, softened**
- **¾ cup (160 g) cream cheese**
- **1 tsp vanilla extract**

1. Measure the icing sugar into a large bowl and set aside.
2. In the bowl of a stand mixer fitted with a paddle attachment, beat the butter and cream cheese on medium speed for 2–3 minutes.
3. Stop the mixer and scrape down the sides of the bowl. With the mixer on low speed, gradually add the icing sugar. Mix until well combined, then add the vanilla. Continue to mix on low for about a minute.
4. Stop the mixer, scrape down the sides of the bowl, then turn the mixer to medium-high speed and beat for 5 minutes. Turn off the mixer, scrape down the sides of the bowl again, then resume mixing at medium-high speed for an additional 2–5 minutes or until it is light and fluffy to the touch.
5. Use buttercream frosting as directed in the recipe.
6. Place any leftover buttercream frosting in an airtight container and store in the fridge for up to 5 days or in the freezer for up to 3 months.

NOTE: To determine when your buttercream frosting is ready, scoop a small amount onto your spatula, then gently tap it against the side of the bowl. If the buttercream frosting easily falls off the spatula, it is ready. If it stays on the spatula, continue mixing on medium-high speed until it reaches the desired consistency.

Peanut Butter Buttercream Frosting

Makes: About 3½ cups | Prep Time: 15–20 minutes

If you love peanut butter and chocolate, make this buttercream frosting to top chocolate cupcakes and cakes, or to sandwich between dark chocolate cookies. If you are a peanut butter purist, use as a frosting on vanilla cake or cupcakes!

INGREDIENTS:

- **4 cups (500 g) icing sugar**
- **½ cup (120 g) whipping cream**
- **1¼ cups (280 g) butter, softened**
- **1 cup (225 g) peanut butter**

1. Measure the icing sugar into a large bowl and set aside.
2. Measure the whipping cream into a glass measuring cup or small bowl and set aside. Measure the peanut butter and set aside.
3. In the bowl of a stand mixer fitted with a paddle attachment, beat the butter on medium speed for 2–3 minutes.
4. Stop the mixer and scrape down the sides of the bowl. With the mixer on low speed, gradually add the icing sugar. Mix until well combined, then slowly add the whipping cream. Continue to mix on low for about a minute. Add the peanut butter and continue to mix on low for about another minute.
5. Stop the mixer, scrape down the sides of the bowl, then turn the mixer to medium-high speed and beat for 5 minutes. Turn off the mixer, scrape down the sides of the bowl again, then resume mixing at medium-high speed for an additional 5–10 minutes or until it is light and fluffy to the touch.
6. Use buttercream frosting as directed in the recipe.
7. Place any leftover buttercream frosting in an airtight container and store in the fridge for up to 5 days or in the freezer for up to 3 months.

NOTE: To determine when your buttercream frosting is ready, scoop a small amount onto your spatula, then gently tap it against the side of the bowl. If the buttercream frosting easily falls off the spatula, it is ready. If it stays on the spatula, continue mixing on medium-high speed until it reaches the desired consistency.

Browned Butter Buttercream Frosting

Makes: About 3 cups | Prep Time: 15–20 minutes

Incorporating browned butter into any recipe enhances the flavour by adding a rich, nutty caramel flavour. When added to our original vanilla buttercream frosting, it elevates the taste to a whole new level of deliciousness. Use it to top any flavour of cake, but it pairs exceptionally well with our banana and chocolate cakes.

RECIPE REQUIRED:
Browned Butter (pg 49)

INGREDIENTS:

- **4¼ cups (560 g) icing sugar**
- **½ cup (120 g) whipping cream**
- **2 tsp vanilla extract**
- **½ cup + 2 Tbsp (145 g) butter, softened**
- **½ cup + 2 Tbsp (145 g) browned butter**

1. Measure the icing sugar into a large bowl and set aside.
2. Measure the whipping cream and vanilla into a glass measuring cup or small bowl and set aside.
3. In the bowl of a stand mixer fitted with a paddle attachment, beat the butter and browned butter on medium speed for 2–3 minutes.
4. Stop the mixer and scrape down the sides of the bowl. With the mixer on low speed, gradually add the icing sugar, then slowly add the whipping cream and vanilla. Continue to mix on low for about a minute or until it is well combined.
5. Stop the mixer, scrape down the sides of the bowl, then turn the mixer to medium-high speed and beat for 5 minutes. Turn off the mixer, scrape down the sides of the bowl again, then resume mixing at medium-high speed for an additional 5–10 minutes or until it is light and fluffy to the touch.
6. Use buttercream frosting as directed in the recipe.
7. Place any leftover buttercream frosting in an airtight container and store in the fridge for up to 5 days or in the freezer for up to 3 months.

NOTE: To determine when your buttercream frosting is ready, scoop a small amount of buttercream frosting onto your spatula, then gently tap it against the side of the bowl. If the buttercream frosting easily falls off the spatula, it is ready. If it stays on the spatula, continue mixing on medium-high speed until it reaches the desired consistency.

Coffee Buttercream Frosting

Makes: About 3 cups | Prep Time: 20–30 minutes + 1 day

This buttercream tastes like a latte. While it's delicious on any flavour of cupcake, we like to spice things up for Thanksgiving by pairing it with our Pumpkin Spice Latte Cupcake (pg 101).

NOTE: This is a 2-stage process. The coffee beans need to steep in whipping cream overnight.

INGREDIENTS:

- **2 Tbsp (15 g) coffee beans**
- **½ cup (120 g) whipping cream**
- **4¼ cups (560 g) icing sugar**
- **1¼ cups (280 g) butter, softened**

Stage 1

1. Measure the coffee beans, and place into a medium sized heat-proof bowl.
2. Add the whipping cream to a medium-sized saucepan and bring to a boil over medium heat.
3. Pour the cream immediately over the coffee beans, then stir with a spatula and allow to cool. Cover the mixture and place in the refrigerator for at least 24 hours.

Stage 2

1. Remove the coffee bean mixture from the refrigerator and stir with a spatula. Place a mesh strainer over a glass measuring cup or bowl and pour the mixture into the cup to remove the beans. Set the strained cream aside.
2. Measure the icing sugar into a large bowl and set aside.
3. In the bowl of a stand mixer fitted with a paddle attachment, beat the butter on medium speed for 2–3 minutes.
4. Stop the mixer and scrape down the sides of the bowl. With the mixer on low speed, gradually add the icing sugar, then slowly add the coffee-steeped cream. Continue to mix on low for about a minute or until it is well combined.
5. Stop the mixer, scrape down the sides of the bowl, then turn the mixer to medium-high speed and beat for 5 minutes. Turn off the mixer and scrape down the sides of the bowl again. Resume mixing at medium-high speed for an additional 5–10 minutes or until it is light and fluffy to the touch. >>

6. Use buttercream frosting as directed in the recipe.
7. Place any leftover buttercream frosting in an airtight container and store in the fridge for up to 5 days or in the freezer for up to 3 months.

NOTE: To determine when your buttercream frosting is ready, scoop a small amount onto your spatula, then gently tap it against the side of the bowl. If the buttercream frosting easily falls off the spatula, it is ready. If it stays on the spatula, continue mixing on medium-high speed until it reaches the desired consistency.

Brown Sugar Buttercream Frosting

Makes: Enough to ice one 9- × 13-inch cake (in its pan) | Prep Time: 1–1½ hours (includes cooling time)

This buttercream frosting, when paired with chocolate cake, is the *original* recipe that inspired us to start Crave. It's perfect for spreading atop a 9- × 13-inch pan of cake but isn't suitable for frosting a two-layer cake or cupcakes (believe us, we tried). Forever cherished, this buttercream frosting remains one of our favourite toppings for the chocolate cakes we bring to friends' and family gatherings.

INGREDIENTS:

- **½ cup (113 g) butter**
- **¾ cup (150 g) brown sugar**
- **⅓ cup (70 g) whipping cream**
- **1 cup (130 g) icing sugar**
- **½ cup (75 g) all-purpose flour**

1. Place the butter and brown sugar in a medium-sized saucepan and set on the stovetop on medium-high heat.
2. Stir, using a heatproof spatula, until all the butter and sugar have melted and the mixture just begins to boil.
3. Remove the saucepan from the heat and add the whipping cream. Transfer the mixture into a medium-sized bowl and allow to cool for 30–60 minutes.
4. Add the icing sugar and flour to the bowl. Using a hand-held mixer, beat on medium-high speed until all the ingredients are combined and the buttercream frosting is smooth and shiny.
5. Use immediately.

Mix-in Buttercream Frostings

The following recipes all start with a vanilla buttercream base, which serves as the foundation for adding various ingredients to create fun flavour combinations.
Feel free to unleash your creativity and experiment with your own mix-ins to create your very own signature buttercream frostings.

Cookies and Cream Buttercream Frosting

Makes: Just under 4 cups | Prep Time: 5–10 minutes

One of the most popular "Cravings of the Month" in our bakeries, this may become your go-to buttercream.

INGREDIENTS:

- **3½ cups (800 g) or 1 batch Vanilla Buttercream Frosting (pg 56)**
- **⅔ cup (150 g) Chocolate Cookie Crumbs (pg 38)**

1. Add the prepared vanilla buttercream frosting to a large-sized bowl. Using a spatula, mix the prepared chocolate cookie crumbs into the buttercream until they are just combined.
2. Use buttercream as directed in the recipe.
3. Place any leftover buttercream in an airtight container and store in the fridge for up to 5 days or in the freezer for up to 3 months.

Caramel Buttercream Frosting

Makes: Just under 4 cups | Prep Time: 5–10 minutes

We love to use this frosting on chocolate and vanilla cupcakes and cakes, but it also pairs especially well with our Apple Cake (pg 91) in the fall.

INGREDIENTS:

- **3½ cups (800 g) or 1 batch Vanilla Buttercream Frosting (pg 56)**
- **⅔ cup (160 g) Caramel Sauce (pg 51)**

1. Add the prepared vanilla buttercream frosting to a large-sized bowl. Using a spatula, mix the prepared caramel sauce into the buttercream until just combined.
2. Use buttercream as directed in the recipe.
3. Place any leftover buttercream frosting in an airtight container and store in the fridge for up to 5 days or in the freezer for up to 3 months.

Toffee Pecan Buttercream Frosting

Makes: About 4 cups | Prep Time: 20–30 minutes | Bake Time: 5–10 minutes

This delicious buttercream frosting is sweet and toasty. It was created to use as the filling for our Pecan Sandwich Cookies (pg 137).

INGREDIENTS:

- **⅔ cup (80 g) pecan pieces, toasted**
- **3½ cups (800 g) or 1 batch of Vanilla Buttercream Frosting (pg 56)**
- **⅔ cup (160 g) Toffee Sauce (pg 41)**

1. Position a rack in the centre of your oven and preheat it to 350°F. Line a cookie sheet with parchment paper.
2. Place the pecan pieces on the cookie sheet and toast in the oven for 5–8 minutes. Allow to cool for at least 10–20 minutes.
3. Add the prepared vanilla buttercream frosting to a large-sized bowl. Using a spatula, mix the prepared toffee sauce into the buttercream until just combined.
4. Fold in pecan pieces.
5. Use buttercream as directed in the recipe.
6. Place any leftover buttercream frosting in an airtight container and store in the fridge for up to 5 days or in the freezer for up to 3 months.

Cupcakes & Cakes

Following are the cupcake and cake recipes our bakeries have been baking from scratch every morning for over 20 years. They include our three base recipes—chocolate, vanilla, and red velvet—as well as some of our favourite cakes we have created for what we refer to as the "Craving of the Month." Since the inception of our business, we've introduced a featured flavour (sometimes two!) each month to add variety to our everyday cupcake and cake menu. All the recipes are designed to make two 8-inch cakes, 18–24 cupcakes, or a 9- × 13-inch sheet cake. Cake and cupcake decorating how-tos are found starting on page 14.

Chocolate Cake with Crave-o-licious Buttercream Frosting

Makes: Two 8-inch cakes | Prep Time: 20–30 minutes | Bake Time: 25–30 minutes
Decorating Time: 30–40 minutes

This chocolate cake is the recipe that inspired us to start Crave. It holds a special place in our hearts, as it has been baked for birthdays, anniversaries, dessert for family Sunday suppers, and to share with friends. This is the only chocolate cake recipe we use, and we firmly believe it's the only one you'll ever need. Until now, it's been a closely guarded secret, shared with only a few close friends. We're excited to finally share it with you and hope you'll love it as much as we do.

RECIPES REQUIRED:

Crave-o-licious Buttercream Frosting (pg 57)

INGREDIENTS:

- **2½ cups (375 g) all-purpose flour**
- **2 cups (400 g) granulated sugar**
- **½ cup (60 g) cocoa powder, sifted**
- **2 tsp baking powder**
- **2 tsp baking soda**
- **¾ tsp salt**
- **⅔ cup (140 g) canola oil**
- **2 eggs**
- **2 tsp vanilla extract**
- **2 cups (500 g) boiling water**

1. Position a rack in the centre of your oven and preheat it to 350°F. Butter two 8-inch round cake pans and place parchment paper at the bottom of each pan.
2. Start boiling water by turning on your kettle.
3. In the bowl of a stand mixer fitted with a paddle attachment, add the flour, sugar, cocoa powder, baking powder, baking soda, and salt. Turn mixer to low speed to combine the ingredients.
4. Stop the mixer and add the canola oil, eggs, and vanilla. Mix for 30 seconds. Turn the mixer to low speed, pour in the boiling water, and mix for another 30 seconds. Stop the mixer, scrape the bowl, and mix at medium speed for 1½ minutes.
5. Divide the batter equally among the two prepared pans. Bake the cakes for 25–30 minutes or until a toothpick inserted into the centre comes out clean.
6. Allow the cakes to cool for 10 minutes, then carefully remove them from the pans and transfer them to a wire rack to cool completely (about an hour) before frosting.
7. While the cakes are cooling, prepare the Crave-o-licious buttercream frosting, then follow the instructions for How to Ice a Two-Layer Cake (pg 18).

>>

Variations

CUPCAKES: Line two cupcake tins with cupcake papers. Transfer the chocolate batter into a glass measuring cup (it will not all fit) and pour the batter into the prepared pans, filling each well about two-thirds full. Bake for 14–18 minutes.

SHEET CAKE: Butter a 9- × 13-inch cake pan and place parchment paper at the bottom of the pan. Transfer the batter into the prepared pan and bake for 25–30 minutes or until a toothpick inserted into the centre comes out clean.

Clockwise from top left:

Chocolate Cake with Mint Buttercream Frosting (pg 75, 57)

Chocolate Cupcake with Cookies and Cream Buttercream Frosting (pg 75, 67)

Chocolate Sheet Cake with Brown Sugar Buttercream Frosting (pg 75, 66)

Chocolate Cupcake with Chocolate Buttercream Frosting (pg 75, 59)

Vanilla Sheet Cake with Strawberry Buttercream Frosting

Makes: One 9- × 13-inch cake | *Prep Time: 20–30 minutes* | *Bake Time: 25–30 minutes*
Decorating Time: 30–40 minutes

This is our mom's vanilla cake recipe; it is cherished and reserved for special occasions, as it requires a little more effort than our chocolate cake! We use this base recipe to craft some of our favourite "Cravings of the Month" by adding fruit or spices or even substituting the milk with eggnog at Christmas.

RECIPES REQUIRED:

Strawberry Buttercream Frosting (pg 60)

INGREDIENTS:

- **2¼ cups (335 g) all-purpose flour**
- **1 Tbsp baking powder**
- **½ tsp salt**
- **½ cup (113 g) butter, softened**
- **1¼ cups (250 g) granulated sugar**
- **2 eggs**
- **2 tsp vanilla extract**
- **1 cup (250 g) milk**

1 Position a rack in the centre of your oven and preheat it to 350°F. Butter a 9- × 13-inch cake pan and place parchment paper at the bottom of the pan.

2 In a medium-sized bowl, add the flour, baking powder, and salt. Whisk to combine and set aside.

3 In the bowl of a stand mixer fitted with a paddle attachment, beat the butter on medium speed for about a minute. Gradually add the sugar. Stop the mixer and use a spatula to scrape the sides of the bowl. Continue mixing on medium-high speed for 5–8 minutes or until the mixture becomes pale and fluffy.

4 Crack the eggs into a small bowl, turn the mixer to low, and add the eggs one by one, then add the vanilla. Mix for 30 seconds. Stop the mixer and scrape the mixing bowl, then turn the mixer to medium-high speed and mix for about a minute or until everything is well combined.

5 Stop the mixer, scrape the bowl again, then turn it to low speed. Add about ½ of the flour mixture, allow to combine, then add the milk and mix until combined. Add the remaining flour mixture and mix on low until everything is combined. Turn mixer to medium speed and mix for 2 more minutes or until a smooth batter forms.

6 Transfer the batter into the prepared pan. Bake the cake for 25–30 minutes or until a toothpick inserted into the centre comes out clean.

>>

7 Let the cake cool for 10 minutes. If desired, remove the cake from the pan and transfer it to a wire rack to cool completely (about an hour) before frosting.

8 While the cake is cooling, prepare the strawberry buttercream frosting, then ice the cake with an offset spatula.

Variations

CUPCAKES: Line two cupcake tins with cupcake papers. Using a cookie scoop or spoon, scoop the batter into the prepared pans filling each well about two-thirds full. Bake for 14–18 minutes.

LAYER CAKE: Butter two 8-inch round cake pans and place parchment paper at the bottom of each pan. Divide the batter equally between the prepared pans and bake the cakes for 26–30 minutes or until a toothpick inserted into the centre comes out clean.

Clockwise from top left:

Vanilla Cupcake with Chocolate Buttercream Frosting (pg 79, 59)

Vanilla Cake with Vanilla Buttercream Frosting (pg 79, 56)

Vanilla Cake with Vava Vanilla Buttercream Frosting (pg 79, 57)

Vanilla Cupcakes with Lemon Buttercream Frosting (pg 79, 58)

Red Velvet Cupcakes with Cream Cheese Buttercream Frosting

Makes: 18–24 cupcakes | Prep Time: 30–40 minutes | Bake Time: 15–20 minutes
Decorating Time: 10–30 minutes

When we first opened Crave, red velvet cupcakes were not on the menu. However, after numerous customer requests, we headed to the kitchen to start testing. We launched our red velvet cupcake early in 2007, and this is the recipe we have been using ever since.

RECIPES REQUIRED:

Cream Cheese Buttercream Frosting (pg 61)

INGREDIENTS:

- **1 cup (250 g) buttermilk***
- **⅔ cup (140 g) canola oil**
- **2 eggs**
- **1 tsp vanilla extract**
- **10 drops super red gel food colouring**
- **2 cups (300 g) all-purpose flour**
- **1½ cups (300 g) granulated sugar**
- **1½ Tbsp cocoa powder, sifted**
- **1 tsp baking soda**
- **1 tsp salt**
- **1 tsp vinegar**

1. Position a rack in the centre of your oven and preheat it to 350°F. Line two cupcake tins with cupcake papers.
2. In a medium-sized bowl, add the buttermilk, oil, eggs, vanilla, and food colouring. Combine with a whisk and set aside.
3. In the bowl of a stand mixer fitted with a paddle attachment, add the flour, sugar, cocoa powder, baking soda, and salt. Turn mixer to low speed to combine the ingredients.
4. Slowly add the oil mixture to the flour mixture. Mix for 30 seconds. Add the vinegar and continue mixing for another 30 seconds. Stop the mixer, scrape down the sides of the bowl, then turn the mixer to medium-high speed and beat for 2 minutes.
5. Transfer the batter into a glass measuring cup (it will not all fit) and pour the batter into the prepared pans, filling each well about two-thirds full. Bake for 15–20 minutes or until a toothpick inserted into the centres comes out clean.
6. Let the cupcakes cool for 10 minutes, then carefully remove them from the pans and transfer them to a wire rack to cool completely (about half an hour) before frosting.
7. While the cupcakes are cooling, prepare the cream cheese buttercream frosting, then follow the instructions for How to Pipe Buttercream Frosting onto Cupcakes (pg 16).

>>

* *If you do not have buttermilk on hand, make your own by adding 1 Tbsp of lemon juice or vinegar to a glass measuring cup, then fill with regular milk to make one cup. Let stand for 5 minutes, stir, then use as you would regular buttermilk. It will not be quite the same as real buttermilk, but it can be used in a pinch!*

Variations

LAYER CAKE: Butter two 8-inch round cake pans and place parchment paper at the bottom of each pan. Divide the batter equally between the two prepared pans and bake the cakes for 30–35 minutes or until a toothpick inserted into the centre comes out clean.

SHEET CAKE: Butter a 9- × 13-inch cake pan and place parchment paper at the bottom of the pan. Transfer the batter into the prepared pan and bake for 30–35 minutes or until a toothpick inserted into the centre comes out clean.

Confetti Cake with Vanilla Buttercream Frosting

Makes: Two 8-inch cakes | Prep Time: 20–30 minutes | Bake Time: 25–30 minutes
Decorating Time: 30–40 minutes

This is a fun variation of our vanilla cake—simply add sprinkles to the batter! While we typically use rainbow sprinkles, feel free to use whatever sprinkles you have on hand.

RECIPES REQUIRED:

Vanilla Buttercream Frosting (pg 56)

INGREDIENTS:

- **2¼ cups (335 g) all-purpose flour**
- **1 Tbsp baking powder**
- **½ tsp salt**
- **½ cup (113 g) butter, softened**
- **1¼ cups (250 g) granulated sugar**
- **2 eggs**
- **2 tsp vanilla extract**
- **1 cup (250 g) milk**
- **2 Tbsp rainbow sprinkles**

1. Position a rack in the centre of your oven and preheat it to 350°F. Butter two 8-inch round cake pans and place parchment paper at the bottom of each pan.
2. In a medium-sized bowl, add the flour, baking powder, and salt. Whisk to combine and set aside.
3. In the bowl of a stand mixer fitted with a paddle attachment, beat the butter on medium speed for about a minute. Gradually add the sugar. Stop the mixer and use a spatula to scrape the sides of the bowl. Continue mixing on medium-high speed for 5–8 minutes or until the mixture becomes pale and fluffy.
4. Crack the eggs into a small bowl, turn the mixer to low, and add the eggs one by one, then add the vanilla. Mix for 30 seconds. Stop the mixer and scrape the sides of the bowl, then turn the mixer to medium-high speed and mix for about a minute or until everything is well combined.
5. Stop the mixer, scrape the bowl again, then turn it to low speed. Add about ½ of the flour mixture, allow to combine, then add the milk and mix until combined. Add the remaining flour mixture and mix on low until everything is combined. Turn mixer to medium speed and mix for 2 more minutes or until a smooth batter forms.
6. Remove the bowl from the mixer and use a spatula to gently fold the sprinkles into the batter.
7. Divide the batter equally between the prepared pans. Bake the cakes for 25–30 minutes or until a toothpick inserted into the centre comes out clean.

>>

8 Let the cakes cool for 10 minutes, then carefully remove them from the pans and transfer them to a wire rack to cool completely (about an hour) before frosting.

9 While the cakes are cooling, prepare the vanilla buttercream, then follow the instructions for How to Ice a Two-Layer Cake (pg 18) and How to Pipe Buttercream Details onto Cakes—Sprinkled Sides (pg 22, 26).

Variations

CUPCAKES: Line two cupcake tins with cupcake papers. Using a cookie scoop or spoon, scoop batter into the prepared pans, filling each well about two-thirds full. Bake for 14–18 minutes.

SHEET CAKE: Butter a 9- × 13-inch cake pan and place parchment paper at the bottom of the pan. Transfer the batter into the prepared pan and bake for 25–30 minutes or until a toothpick inserted into the centre comes out clean.

Carrot Cake with Cream Cheese Buttercream Frosting

Makes: Two 8-inch cakes | Prep Time: 30–40 minutes | Bake Time: 25–30 minutes
Decorating Time: 30–40 minutes

This recipe is a true labour of love. It underwent about 50 iterations before we finalized it for an Easter menu. Our mom's original recipe was delicious as a cake, but didn't yield beautiful cupcakes. So we experimented with her recipe until we found the perfect combination, and we found the secret lies in using equal parts oil and applesauce.

RECIPES REQUIRED:
Cream Cheese Buttercream Frosting (pg 61)

INGREDIENTS:

- **1¾ cups (260 g) all-purpose flour**
- **2 tsp cinnamon**
- **¾ tsp baking powder**
- **¾ tsp baking soda**
- **½ tsp salt**
- **¾ cup (150 g) granulated sugar**
- **¾ cup (150 g) brown sugar**
- **3 eggs**
- **¼ cup (60 g) milk**
- **1 tsp vanilla extract**
- **⅓ cup (85 g) canola oil**
- **⅓ cup (85 g) unsweetened applesauce**
- **2½ cups (350 g) grated carrots, approximately 6 large carrots**

1. Position a rack in the centre of your oven and preheat it to 350°F. Butter two 8-inch round cake pans and place parchment paper at the bottom of each pan.
2. In a medium-sized bowl, add the flour, cinnamon, baking powder, baking soda, and salt. Whisk to combine and set aside.
3. In the bowl of a stand mixer fitted with a paddle attachment, combine the sugars, eggs, milk, and vanilla. Mix on medium speed for about a minute.
4. Stop the mixer and use a spatula to scrape the sides of the bowl. Add the oil and applesauce to the sugar mixture and continue mixing on medium speed for 1–2 minutes or until well combined.
5. Turn the mixer to low speed and add the dry ingredients, continuing to mix for a minute or until a smooth batter forms. Add the carrots and mix until just combined.
6. Divide the batter equally between the two prepared pans. Bake the cakes for 25–30 minutes or until a toothpick inserted into the centre comes out clean.
7. Let the cakes cool for 10 minutes, then carefully remove them from the pans and transfer them to a wire rack to cool completely (about an hour) before frosting.

>>

8 While the cakes are cooling, prepare the cream cheese buttercream, then follow the instructions for How to Ice a Two-Layer Cake (pg 18).

Variations

CUPCAKES: Line two cupcake tins with cupcake papers. Using a cookie scoop or a spoon, scoop batter into the prepared pans, filling each well about two-thirds full. Bake for 14–18 minutes.

SHEET CAKE: Butter a 9- × 13-inch cake pan and place parchment paper at the bottom of the pan. Transfer the batter into the prepared pan and bake for 25–30 minutes or until a toothpick inserted into the centre comes out clean.

LOAF: Make the recipe using three-quarters of the ingredients, then transfer the batter into a prepared 8- × 5-inch loaf pan and bake for 45–60 minutes.

PRO TIP: To ensure accuracy for a three-quarters recipe, be sure to weigh the ingredients.

Apple Cake with Caramel Buttercream Frosting

Makes: Two 8-inch cakes / Prep Time: 45–60 minutes / Bake Time: 30–35 minutes
Decorating Time: 30–40 minutes

We love featuring this apple cake on our fall menu. Though we don't include it every year, it typically shows up in September, coinciding with the arrival of fresh apples at the farmers' markets. This cake is delicious, whether it is served with buttercream, topped with our Farmer's Butter Glaze (pg 40), or simply dusted with icing sugar.

RECIPES REQUIRED:

Caramel Buttercream Frosting (pg 68)
Caramel Sauce (pg 51) (optional)

INGREDIENTS:

- **3½ cups (525 g) all-purpose flour**
- **3 tsp cinnamon**
- **¾ tsp nutmeg**
- **1 tsp baking powder**
- **¾ tsp baking soda**
- **½ tsp salt**
- **1 cup (225 g) butter**
- **¾ cup (150 g) brown sugar**
- **¾ cup (150 g) granulated sugar**
- **2 eggs**
- **2 tsp vanilla extract**
- **3½ cups or 6 small grated apples (we recommend using Ambrosia apples when in season)**

1. Position a rack in the centre of your oven and preheat it to 350°F. Butter two 8-inch round cake pans and place parchment paper at the bottom of each pan.
2. In a large-sized bowl, add the flour, spices, baking powder, baking soda, and salt. Whisk to combine and set aside.
3. In the bowl of a stand mixer fitted with a paddle attachment, beat the butter on medium speed for about a minute. Gradually add the sugars. Stop the mixer and use a spatula to scrape the sides of the bowl. Continue mixing on medium speed for 5–8 minutes or until the mixture becomes pale and fluffy.
4. Crack the eggs into a small bowl, turn the mixer to low, and add the eggs one by one, then add the vanilla. Mix for 30 seconds. Stop the mixer and scrape the mixing bowl, then turn the mixer to medium-high speed and mix for about a minute or until everything is well combined.
5. Stop the mixer, scrape the bowl again, then turn it to low speed, add the flour mixture, and mix until everything is combined. Add the apples and mix until just combined.
6. Divide the batter equally between the prepared pans, and using an offset spatula or the back of a spoon, spread the batter to the edges of the pan. Bake the cakes for 30–35 minutes or until a toothpick inserted into the centre comes out clean.

>>

7 Let the cakes cool for 10 minutes, then carefully remove them from the pans and transfer them to a wire rack to cool completely (about an hour) before frosting.

8 While the cakes are cooling, prepare the caramel buttercream, then follow the instructions for How to Ice a Two-Layer Cake (pg 18).

PRO TIP: If you want to recreate the photo, prepare the Caramel Sauce (pg 51) and pour onto the cake right before serving.

Variations

CUPCAKES: Line two cupcake tins with cupcake papers. Using a cookie scoop or spoon, scoop batter into the prepared pans, filling each well about two-thirds full. Bake for 14–18 minutes.

SHEET CAKE: Butter a 9- × 13-inch cake pan and place parchment paper at the bottom of the pan. Transfer the batter into the prepared pan and bake for 25–30 minutes or until a toothpick inserted into the centre comes out clean

Strawberry Cake with Strawberry Cream Cheese Buttercream Frosting

Makes: Two 8-inch cakes / Prep Time: 2–3 hours / Bake Time: 25–30 minutes
Decorating Time: 30–45 minutes

Creating this cake involves preparing a few recipes, but the result is absolutely worth the effort. Originally created for a Mother's Day menu, this delicious cake makes any special occasion just a little more special.

RECIPE TO PREPARE BEFORE YOU BEGIN:

Graham Cracker Crumbs, coarse (pg 36)

RECIPES REQUIRED:

½ recipe Cream Cheese Buttercream Frosting (pg 61)
½ recipe Strawberry Buttercream Frosting (pg 60)

INGREDIENTS:

- **2¼ cups (335 g) all-purpose flour**
- **1 Tbsp baking powder**
- **½ tsp salt**
- **½ cup (113 g) butter, softened**
- **1¼ cups (250 g) granulated sugar**
- **2 eggs**
- **2 tsp vanilla extract**
- **1 cup (250g) milk**
- **1 cup (175 g) fresh strawberries, chopped into 1-inch pieces**

1 Position a rack in the centre of your oven and preheat it to 350°F. Butter two 8-inch round cake pans and place parchment paper at the bottom of each pan.

2 In a medium-sized bowl, add the flour, baking powder, and salt. Whisk to combine and set aside.

3 In the bowl of a stand mixer fitted with a paddle attachment, beat the butter on medium speed for about a minute. Gradually add the sugar. Stop the mixer and use a spatula to scrape the sides of the bowl. Continue mixing on medium-high speed for 5–8 minutes or until the mixture becomes pale and fluffy.

4 Crack the eggs into a small bowl, turn the mixer to low, add the eggs one by one, then add the vanilla. Mix for 30 seconds. Stop the mixer and scrape the mixing bowl, then turn the mixer to medium-high speed and mix for about a minute or until everything is combined.

5 Stop the mixer, scrape the bowl again, then turn it to low speed. Add about ½ of the flour mixture, allow to combine, then add the milk and mix until combined. Add the remaining flour mixture and mix on low until everything is combined. Turn mixer to medium speed and mix for 2 more minutes or until a smooth batter forms.

6 Remove the bowl from the mixer and use a spatula to gently fold the chopped strawberries into the batter. >>

7 Divide the batter equally between the prepared pans. Bake the cakes for 25–30 minutes or until a toothpick inserted into the centre comes out clean.

8 Let the cakes cool for 10 minutes, then carefully remove them from the pans and transfer them to a wire rack to cool completely (about an hour) before assembling.

9 While the cakes are cooling, prepare the cream cheese buttercream and strawberry buttercream. To make strawberry cream cheese buttercream: mix equal parts of cream cheese buttercream and strawberry buttercream together.

10 Refer to how to Ice a Two-Layer Cake (pg 18) and How to Add Filling to a Layer Cake (pg 20), using the graham cracker crumbs for the filling layer and the strawberry cream cheese buttercream for the frosting.

Banana Caramel Cupcakes with Browned Butter Buttercream Frosting

Makes: 18–24 cupcakes | Prep Time: 30–40 minutes | Bake Time: 20–25 minutes
Decorating Time: 30–45 minutes

These delicious cupcakes take the humble banana to new heights. A light banana cupcake filled with caramel and topped with browned butter buttercream frosting is perfect for a cozy family gathering or a sweet personal treat.

RECIPES TO PREPARE BEFORE YOU BEGIN:

Browned Butter (pg 49)
½ recipe Caramel Filling (pg 50)

RECIPES REQUIRED:

Browned Butter Buttercream Frosting (pg 63)

INGREDIENTS:

- **2 ripe bananas, mashed**
- **½ cup (130 g) sour cream**
- **1½ cups (220 g) all-purpose flour**
- **2 tsp baking powder**
- **½ tsp salt**
- **¾ cup (170 g) butter**
- **1¼ cups (250 g) granulated sugar**
- **2 eggs**
- **¾ tsp vanilla extract**

1. Position a rack in the centre of your oven and preheat it to 350°F. Line two cupcake tins with cupcake papers. In a small bowl, mix together the bananas and sour cream and set aside.
2. In a medium-sized bowl, add the flour, baking powder, and salt. Whisk to combine and set aside.
3. In the bowl of a stand mixer fitted with a paddle attachment, beat the butter on medium speed for about a minute. Gradually add the sugar. Stop the mixer and use a spatula to scrape the sides of the bowl. Continue mixing on medium speed for 5–8 minutes or until the mixture becomes pale and fluffy.
4. Crack the eggs into a small bowl, turn the mixer to low, and add the eggs one by one, then add the vanilla. Mix for 30 seconds. Stop the mixer and scrape the bowl, then turn the mixer to medium-high speed and mix for about a minute or until everything is well combined.
5. Stop the mixer, scrape down the sides of the bowl, and continue to mix on low speed. Slowly add the banana and sour cream mixture. Turn the mixer to medium speed and continue to mix for about a minute or until well combined. (The mixture may split, and that is okay.)
6. Turn the mixer to low speed and slowly add the flour mixture. Turn the mixer to medium speed and continue to mix for 2 minutes or until well combined.

>>

7 Using a cookie scoop or spoon, scoop the batter into the prepared pans, filling each well about two-thirds full. Bake the cupcakes for 20–25 minutes or until a toothpick inserted into the centres comes out clean.

8 Let the cupcakes cool for 10 minutes, then carefully remove them from the pans and transfer them to a wire rack to cool completely (about half an hour) before frosting.

9 While the cupcakes are cooling, prepare the browned butter buttercream frosting. Then refer to How to Fill a Cupcake with Filling or Buttercream (pg 27), using the caramel filling and the browned butter buttercream for icing the cupcakes.

Variations

LAYER CAKE: Butter two 8-inch round cake pans and place parchment paper at the bottom of each pan. Divide the batter equally between the two prepared pans. Bake the cakes for 26–30 minutes or until a toothpick inserted into the centre comes out clean. Follow the instructions for How to Ice a Two-Layer Cake (pg 18) and How to Add Filling to a Layer Cake (pg 20) using the caramel filling.

SHEET CAKE: Butter a 9- × 13-inch cake pan and place parchment paper at the bottom of the pan. Transfer the batter into the prepared pan and bake for 25–30 minutes or until a toothpick inserted into the centre comes out clean. (Omit the caramel filling.)

Pumpkin Spice Latte Cupcakes with Coffee Buttercream Frosting

Makes: 18–24 cupcakes | Prep Time: 30–40 min | Bake Time: 15–20 minutes
Decorating Time: 30–45 minutes

A Thanksgiving classic, you'll find our bakeries filled with pumpkin cupcakes every October. We switch up the buttercream frosting from year to year. For this recipe we used our Coffee Buttercream, but you can also pair these cupcakes with our classic Cream Cheese Buttercream.

RECIPES REQUIRED:

Coffee Buttercream Frosting (pg 64) (Requires 1 day of advance prep)

INGREDIENTS:

- **3 cups (450 g) all-purpose flour**
- **2 tsp baking powder**
- **1 tsp baking soda**
- **2½ tsp cinnamon**
- **1½ tsp cardamom**
- **1½ tsp ginger**
- **¼ tsp cloves**
- **1 tsp salt**
- **4 eggs**
- **2 Tbsp oil**
- **2 tsp vanilla extract**
- **1¾ cups (400 g) pumpkin purée**
- **½ cup (130 g) sour cream**
- **¾ cup (170 g) butter, softened**
- **2¼ cups (450 g) brown sugar**

1. Position a rack in the centre of your oven and preheat it to 350°F. Line two cupcake tins with cupcake papers.
2. In a large-sized bowl, add the flour, baking powder, baking soda, all the spices, and the salt. Whisk to combine and set aside.
3. In a small bowl, add the eggs, oil, and vanilla. Whisk to combine and set aside.
4. In a large-sized bowl, add the pumpkin purée and sour cream. Whisk to combine and set aside.
5. In the bowl of a stand mixer fitted with a paddle attachment, beat the butter on medium speed for about a minute. Gradually add the brown sugar. Stop the mixer and use a spatula to scrape the sides of the bowl. Continue mixing on medium speed for 5–8 minutes or until the mixture becomes pale and fluffy.
6. Stop the mixer, scrape down the bowl, and continue to mix on low speed. Slowly add the egg and oil mixture. Turn mixer to medium speed and continue to mix for about a minute until well combined.
7. Stop the mixer, scrape the bowl again, then turn to low speed. Add about ½ the flour mixture and allow to combine, then add the pumpkin sour cream mixture and mix until combined. Add the remaining flour and mix on low until everything is thoroughly combined. Turn mixer to medium speed and mix for 2 more minutes until all the ingredients are fully combined. >>

8. Using a cookie scoop or spoon, scoop batter into the prepared pans, filling each well about two-thirds full. Bake for 15–20 minutes or until a toothpick inserted into the centres comes out clean.
9. Let the cupcakes cool for 10 minutes, then carefully remove them from the pans and transfer them to a wire rack to cool completely (about half an hour) before frosting.
10. While the cupcakes are cooling, prepare the coffee buttercream frosting, then follow the instructions for How to Pipe Buttercream Frosting onto Cupcakes (pg 16).

Variations

LAYER CAKE: Butter two 8-inch round cake pans and place parchment paper at the bottom of each pan. Divide the batter equally among the two prepared pans. Bake the cakes for 26–30 minutes or until a toothpick inserted into the centre comes out clean.

SHEET CAKE: Butter a 9- × 13-inch cake pan and place parchment paper at the bottom of the pan. Transfer the batter into the prepared pan and bake for 25–30 minutes or until a toothpick inserted into the centre comes out clean.

Our Bakery Cupcake Menu

COCONUT CHOCOLATE

Chocolate Cupcake (pg 75) with Vanilla Buttercream (pg 56) rolled in coconut

NUTTY OVER CHOCOLATE

Chocolate Cupcake (pg 75) with Peanut Butter Buttercream (pg 62)

STRAWBERRY CHOCOLATE

Chocolate Cupcake (pg 75) with Strawberry Buttercream (pg 60)

VAVA VANILLA

Vanilla Cupcake (pg 79) with VaVa Vanilla Buttercream (pg 57)

LEMON

Vanilla Cupcake (pg 79) with Lemon Buttercream (pg 58)

COCONUT VANILLA

Vanilla Cupcake (pg 79) with Vanilla Buttercream (pg 56) rolled in coconut

CRAVE-O-LICIOUS

Chocolate Cupcake (pg 75) with Crave-o-licious Buttercream (pg 57)

DIRTY BLONDE

Vanilla Cupcake (pg 79) with Chocolate Buttercream (pg 59)

MINT CHIP

Chocolate Cupcake (pg 75) with Mint Buttercream (pg 57)

RED VELVET

Red Velvet Cupcake (pg 83) with Cream Cheese Buttercream (pg 61)

STRAWBERRY VANILLA

Vanilla Cupcake (pg 79) with Strawberry Buttercream (pg 60)

DARK ANGEL

Chocolate Cupcake (pg 75) with Cream Cheese Buttercream (pg 61)

JUST CHOCOLATE

Chocolate Cupcake (pg 75) with Chocolate Buttercream (pg 59)

Cookies & Bars

Although Crave is known for creating the best cupcakes, we also make delicious cookies and bars. This chapter is filled with our favourite recipes, including both drop and rolled cookies as well as a few of our most popular bars.

A FEW *tips* AND *tricks* FOR MAKING, BAKING, AND STORING COOKIES:

- Each cookie recipe can be doubled if you use a stand mixer.
- To reduce the amount of time you spend baking cookies, use the convection setting on your oven and set the temperature to 325°F. This allows you to bake three trays of cookies at a time.
- Freeze baked cookies for up to 3 months.
- If you don't have time to bake all the cookie dough, scoop any remaining dough onto a cookie sheet and refrigerate until firm to the touch. Transfer the dough balls to an airtight container or zip-lock bag and freeze for up to 3 months.
- If you have a dessert emergency or are simply craving a cookie, bake frozen dough balls using the same method as regular cookies, adjusting the baking time as needed.

PRO TIP FOR PERFECTLY BAKED COOKIES: Set the timer to half the required baking time. Then rotate your pans front to back and switch their rack positions in the oven. Then set your timer for the remaining recommended time or until the cookies are golden brown.

Salted Chocolate Chunk Cookies

Makes: About 40 cookies | Prep Time: 30–40 minutes | Bake Time: 10–12 minutes

Our salted chocolate chunk cookies aren't just cookies; they're an experience, a testament to the love and dedication we put into crafting the perfect sweet indulgence. Every time we see a recipe titled Best Chocolate Chip Cookie, we try it. Without fail, we can attest these are the very best chocolate chip cookies!

INGREDIENTS:

- **3 cups (450 g) all-purpose flour**
- **1 tsp baking soda**
- **½ tsp baking powder**
- **½ tsp salt**
- **1 cup (225 g) butter**
- **¾ cup (150 g) granulated sugar**
- **¾ cup (150 g) firmly packed brown sugar**
- **2 eggs**
- **1 tsp vanilla extract**
- **1 cup (200 g) dark chocolate chunks**
- **1 cup (200 g) chocolate, roughly chopped (we use 66 percent Valrhona Chocolate)**
- **2 tsp flaky sea salt (optional)**

1. Position a rack in the centre of your oven and preheat it to 350°F. Line cookie sheets with parchment paper.
2. In a medium-sized bowl, add the flour, baking soda, baking powder, and salt. Whisk to combine and set aside.
3. In the bowl of a stand mixer fitted with a paddle attachment, beat the butter on medium speed for about a minute. Gradually add the sugars. Stop the mixer and scrape the sides of the bowl with a spatula. Continue mixing on medium-high speed for 5–8 minutes or until the mixture becomes pale and fluffy.
4. Crack the eggs into a small bowl. Turn the mixer to low and add the eggs one by one, then add the vanilla. Mix for 30 seconds. Stop the mixer and scrape the mixing bowl, then turn the mixer to medium-high speed and mix for about a minute or until everything is well combined.
5. Stop the mixer, scrape the bowl, and continue mixing on low speed. Slowly add the flour mixture and mix for 1–2 minutes or until well combined. Then add the chocolate chips and chopped chocolate and mix until just combined.
6. Using a cookie scoop, drop the scoops of dough onto the prepared cookie sheets about 2 inches apart. If desired, sprinkle the top of each cookie with the flaky sea salt.
7. Bake for 10–12 minutes or until golden brown.
8. Allow the cookies to cool on the baking sheets for 5 minutes, then transfer them to a wire rack to cool completely.

Oatmeal Milk Chocolate Toffee Cookies

Makes: About 50 cookies | Prep Time: 30–40 minutes | Bake Time: 10–12 minutes
Dipping Time: 10–15 minutes

This is a customer favourite in the bakeries. We dip the cookies in milk chocolate and sprinkle extra toffee bits on top. However, the dip is not required for the cookies to taste delicious.

INGREDIENTS:

- **3¼ cups (320 g) large-flake oatmeal**
- **1½ cups (225 g) all-purpose flour**
- **1 tsp baking soda**
- **½ tsp baking powder**
- **¾ tsp salt**
- **1 cup (225 g) butter**
- **¾ cup (150 g) granulated sugar**
- **¾ cup (150 g) firmly packed brown sugar**
- **2 eggs**
- **1 tsp vanilla extract**
- **1¾ cups (250 g) milk chocolate chips**
- **½ cup (85 g) toffee bits**
- **1 cup (250 g) milk coating chocolate (optional, for the dip)**

Variation

OATMEAL CHOCOLATE CHIP COOKIES: After step 5, instead of the milk chocolate chips and toffee bits, add 2 cups (400 g) of dark chocolate chips.

1. Position a rack in the centre of your oven and preheat it to 350°F. Line cookie sheets with parchment paper.
2. In a medium-sized bowl, add the oatmeal, flour, baking soda, baking powder, and salt. Whisk to combine and set aside.
3. In the bowl of a stand mixer fitted with a paddle attachment, beat the butter on medium speed for about a minute. Gradually add the sugars. Stop the mixer and use a spatula to scrape the sides of the bowl. Continue mixing on medium-high speed for 5–8 minutes or until the mixture becomes pale and fluffy.
4. Crack the eggs into a small bowl. Turn the mixer to low and add the eggs one by one, then add the vanilla. Mix for 30 seconds. Stop the mixer and scrape the mixing bowl, then turn the mixer to medium-high speed and mix for about a minute or until everything is well combined.
5. Stop the mixer, scrape the bowl, and continue to mix on low speed. Slowly add the oatmeal mixture and mix for about 2 minutes or until well combined. Then add the milk chocolate and toffee bits and mix until just combined.
6. Using a cookie scoop, drop the scoops of dough onto the prepared cookie sheets about 2 inches apart.
7. Bake for 10–12 minutes or until golden brown.
8. Allow the cookies to cool on the baking sheets for 5 minutes, transfer them to a wire rack to cool completely, then follow the instructions for How to Dip and Drizzle Cookies (pg 28).

Double Chocolate Sandwich Cookies

Makes: About 40 cookies | Prep Time: 30–40 minutes | Bake Time: 10–12 minutes
Decorating Time: 10–15 minutes

This recipe is inspired by a biscotti recipe our mom used to make at Christmas time. In the bakeries, you will always find the original: two dark chocolate cookies sandwiched with Cream Cheese Buttercream Frosting. This is our classic combination; however, any of the buttercream frosting recipes in this book can be used as a filling. A few of our favourites include chocolate, strawberry, and mint.

RECIPES REQUIRED:

Cream Cheese Buttercream Frosting (pg 61)

INGREDIENTS:

- **2½ cups (375 g) all-purpose flour**
- **1¼ cups (150 g) cocoa powder, sifted**
- **1 tsp baking soda**
- **¾ tsp salt**
- **1 cup (225 g) butter**
- **1 cup (200 g) granulated sugar**
- **1 cup (200 g) firmly packed brown sugar**
- **2 eggs**
- **2 tsp vanilla extract**

1. Position a rack in the centre of your oven and preheat it to 350°F. Line cookie sheets with parchment paper.
2. In a medium-sized bowl, add the flour, cocoa powder, baking soda, and salt. Whisk to combine and set aside.
3. In the bowl of a stand mixer fitted with a paddle attachment, beat the butter on medium speed for about a minute. Gradually add the sugars. Stop the mixer and use a spatula to scrape the sides of the bowl. Continue mixing on medium-high speed for 5–8 minutes or until the mixture becomes pale and fluffy.
4. Crack the eggs into a small bowl. Turn the mixer to low and add the eggs one by one, then add the vanilla. Mix for 30 seconds. Stop the mixer and scrape the mixing bowl, then turn the mixer to medium-high speed and mix for about a minute or until everything is well combined.
5. Stop the mixer, scrape the bowl, and continue to mix on low speed. Slowly add the flour mixture and mix for about 2 minutes or until well combined.
6. Using a cookie scoop, drop the scoops of dough onto the prepared cookie sheets about 2 inches apart.
7. Bake for 10–12 minutes.

>>

Chocolate Cookies shown with Chocolate Buttercream Frosting (pg 59), Cream Cheese Buttercream Frosting (pg 61), Strawberry Buttercream Frosting (pg 60) and Mint Buttercream Frosting (pg 57)

8 Allow the cookies to cool on the baking sheets for 5 minutes, then transfer them to a wire rack to cool completely.

9 While the cookies are cooling, prepare the cream cheese buttercream. Follow the directions for How to Pipe Buttercream Frosting onto Cupcakes (pg 16), but use a #10 round tip, to fill the cookies.

PRO TIP: It can be difficult to determine when dark chocolate cookies are finished baking. Check the cookies a couple of minutes before the timer goes off. You'll notice they still have a sheen on top. The cookies are baked once you no longer see the sheen.

Peanut Butter Milk Chocolate Chip Cookies

Makes: About 30 cookies | Prep Time: 30–40 minutes | Bake Time: 12–14 minutes

A classic cookie, delicious with or without chocolate. We prefer our peanut butter cookies with milk chocolate, but feel free to substitute it with dark chocolate, peanuts, or Reese's Pieces.

INGREDIENTS:

- **1¾ cups (260 g) all-purpose flour**
- **¾ tsp baking soda**
- **¾ tsp salt**
- **½ cup (113 g) butter**
- **¾ cup (200 g) peanut butter**
- **1¼ cups (250 g) firmly packed brown sugar**
- **1 egg**
- **1 tsp vanilla extract**
- **3 Tbsp (50 g) milk**
- **1 cup (200 g) milk chocolate chunks**

1. Position a rack in the centre of your oven and preheat it to 350°F. Line cookie sheets with parchment paper.
2. In a medium-sized bowl, add the flour, baking soda, and salt. Whisk to combine and set aside.
3. In the bowl of a stand mixer fitted with a paddle attachment, beat the butter on medium speed for about a minute. Stop the mixer and add the peanut butter, then continue to mix on medium-high speed. Gradually add the sugar and mix until combined. Stop the mixer and use a spatula to scrape the sides of the bowl. Continue mixing on medium-high speed for 5–8 minutes or until the mixture becomes pale and fluffy.
4. Crack the egg into a small bowl. Turn the mixer to low and add the egg, then add the vanilla. Mix for 30 seconds. Stop the mixer and scrape the mixing bowl, then turn it to medium-high speed and mix for about a minute or until everything is well combined.
5. Stop the mixer, scrape the bowl, and continue to mix on low speed. Slowly add about half the flour mixture, then add the milk, then add the remaining flour mixture and mix for about 2 minutes or until well combined. Add the milk chocolate and mix until just combined.
6. Using a cookie scoop, drop the scoops of dough onto the prepared cookie sheets about 2 inches apart. Using a long-pronged fork, flatten the cookies slightly with a crisscross pattern.
7. Bake for 12–14 minutes or until golden brown.
8. Allow the cookies to cool on the baking sheets for 5 minutes, then transfer them to a wire rack to cool completely.

Confetti Cookies

Makes: About 35 cookies | Prep Time: 30–40 minutes | Bake Time: 10–12 minutes

This is one of the best selling cookies in our bakeries. Add your favourite sprinkles to the dough and you will have a party in a cookie. For extra-fun cookies, roll the dough balls in sprinkles before baking.

INGREDIENTS:

- **3¼ cups (470 g) all-purpose flour**
- **1 tsp baking soda**
- **½ tsp baking powder**
- **½ tsp salt**
- **1 cup (225 g) butter**
- **1¾ cups (350 g) granulated sugar**
- **2 eggs**
- **1 Tbsp vanilla extract**
- **⅓ cup (60 g) rainbow sprinkles**

1. Position a rack in the centre of your oven and preheat it to 350°F. Line cookie sheets with parchment paper.
2. In a medium-sized bowl, add the flour, baking soda, baking powder, and salt. Whisk to combine and set aside.
3. In the bowl of a stand mixer fitted with a paddle attachment, beat the butter on medium speed for about a minute. Gradually add the sugar. Stop the mixer and use a spatula to scrape the sides of the bowl. Continue mixing on medium-high speed for 5–8 minutes or until the mixture becomes pale and fluffy.
4. Crack the eggs into a small bowl. Turn the mixer to low and add the eggs one by one, then add the vanilla. Mix for 30 seconds. Stop the mixer and scrape the mixing bowl, then turn the mixer to medium-high and mix for about a minute or until everything is well combined.
5. Stop the mixer, scrape the bowl, and continue to mix on low speed. Slowly add the flour mixture and mix for about 2 minutes or until well combined. Then add the sprinkles and mix until just combined.
6. Using a cookie scoop, drop the scoops of dough on the cookie sheets about 2 inches apart.
7. Bake for 10–12 minutes, or until lightly golden brown.
8. Allow the cookies to cool on the baking sheets for 5 minutes, then transfer them to a wire rack to cool completely.

Snickerdoodle Cookies

Makes: About 35 cookies | Prep Time: 30–40 minutes | Bake Time: 12–14 minutes

Freshly baked snickerdoodles fill your kitchen with the smells of cinnamon-sugar goodness. These cookies are delicious, and though we usually like to eat our cookies once they have cooled, we make an exception for these ones.

INGREDIENTS:

- **2¾ cups (405 g) all-purpose flour**
- **2 tsp cream of tartar**
- **1 tsp baking soda**
- **½ tsp salt**
- **1¼ cups (280 g) butter**
- **1½ cups (300 g) granulated sugar (reserve ½ cup for cinnamon sugar mixture)**
- **½ cup (100 g) brown sugar**
- **2 eggs**
- **1 tsp vanilla extract**
- **2 Tbsp cinnamon**

1. Position a rack in the centre of your oven and preheat it to 350°F. Line cookie sheets with parchment paper.
2. In a medium-sized bowl, add the flour, cream of tartar, baking soda, and salt. Whisk to combine and set aside.
3. In the bowl of a stand mixer fitted with a paddle attachment, beat the butter on medium speed for about a minute. Gradually add 1 cup of the granulated sugar and the brown sugar. Stop the mixer and use a spatula to scrape the sides of the bowl. Continue mixing on medium-high speed for 5–8 minutes or until the mixture becomes pale and fluffy.
4. Crack the eggs into a small bowl. Turn the mixer to low and add the eggs one by one, then add the vanilla. Mix for 30 seconds. Stop the mixer and scrape the mixing bowl, then turn it to medium-high speed and mix for about a minute or until everything is well combined.
5. Stop the mixer, scrape the bowl, and continue mixing on low speed. Slowly add the flour mixture and mix for 2 minutes or until well combined.
6. In a small bowl, add the remaining ½ cup sugar and the cinnamon and mix to combine. Using a cookie scoop, drop scoops of dough one by one into the bowl of sugar and cinnamon. Use your fingers to roll the dough around the bowl to ensure they are evenly coated. Then place the coated cookie dough balls on the prepared cookie sheets about 2 inches apart.
7. Bake for 12–14 minutes or until golden brown.
8. Allow the cookies to cool on the baking sheets for 5 minutes, then transfer them to a wire rack to cool completely.

Gingersnap Cookies

Makes: About 30 cookies | Prep Time: 30–40 minutes | Bake Time: 10–12 minutes

This classic gingersnap cookie recipe is delicious for enjoying with a cup of tea or coffee. These cookies also taste great sandwiched with vanilla buttercream frosting.

INGREDIENTS:

- **2¼ cups (335 g) all-purpose flour**
- **1 tsp baking soda**
- **2 tsp ground ginger**
- **¾ tsp cinnamon**
- **½ tsp ground cloves**
- **½ tsp salt**
- **¾ cup (165 g) butter**
- **1½ cups (300 g) granulated sugar (reserve ½ cup for coating cookie dough)**
- **¼ cup (75 g) fancy molasses**
- **1 egg**

1. Position a rack in the centre of your oven and preheat it to 350°F. Line cookie sheets with parchment paper.
2. In a medium-sized bowl, add the flour, baking soda, spices, and salt. Whisk to combine and set aside.
3. In the bowl of a stand mixer fitted with a paddle attachment, beat the butter on medium speed for about a minute. Gradually add 1 cup of sugar and the fancy molasses. Stop the mixer and use a spatula to scrape the sides of the bowl. Continue mixing on medium-high speed for 5–8 minutes or until the mixture becomes pale and fluffy.
4. Crack the egg into a small bowl. Turn the mixer to low and add the egg. Stop the mixer and scrape the mixing bowl, then turn it to medium-high speed and mix for about a minute or until everything is well combined.
5. Stop the mixer, scrape the bowl, and continue mixing on low speed. Slowly add the flour mixture and mix for about 2 minutes or until well combined.
6. In a small bowl, add the remaining ½ cup sugar. Using a cookie scoop, drop scoops of dough one by one into the bowl of sugar. Use your fingers to roll the dough around the bowl to ensure they are evenly coated. Then place the coated cookie dough balls on the prepared cookie sheets about 2 inches apart.
7. Bake for 10–12 minutes or until golden brown.
8. Allow the cookies to cool on the baking sheets for 5 minutes, then transfer them to a wire rack to cool completely.

S'more Cookies

Makes: About 45 cookies | Prep Time: 30–40 mins | Bake: 10–12 minutes

Who doesn't love s'mores? You don't have to wait to go camping to enjoy one; you can bake a batch of these delicious cookies at home.

RECIPE TO PREPARE BEFORE YOU BEGIN:

Graham Cracker Crumbs, coarse (pg 36)

INGREDIENTS:

- **1 cup (200 g) milk chocolate chunks**
- **½ cup (100 g) dark chocolate chunks**
- **1½ cups (180 g) graham cracker crumbs, coarse**
- **1¼ cups (60 g) mini marshmallows**
- **3 cups (450 g) all-purpose flour**
- **1 tsp baking soda**
- **½ tsp baking powder**
- **¾ tsp salt**
- **1 cup (225 g) butter**
- **¾ cup (150 g) granulated sugar**
- **¾ cup (150 g) firmly packed brown sugar**
- **2 eggs**
- **1 tsp vanilla extract**

1. Position a rack in the centre of your oven and preheat it to 350°F. Line cookie sheets with parchment paper.
2. In a medium-sized bowl, add the chocolate chunks, graham cracker crumbs, and mini marshmallows and set aside.
3. In a medium-sized bowl, add the flour, baking soda, baking powder, and salt. Whisk to combine and set aside.
4. In the bowl of a stand mixer fitted with a paddle attachment, beat the butter on medium speed for about a minute. Gradually add the sugars. Stop the mixer and use a spatula to scrape the sides of the bowl. Continue mixing on medium-high speed for 5–8 minutes or until the mixture becomes pale and fluffy.
5. Crack the eggs into a small bowl. Turn the mixer to low and add the eggs one by one, then add the vanilla. Mix for 30 seconds. Stop the mixer and scrape the mixing bowl, then turn it to medium-high speed and mix for about a minute or until everything is well combined.
6. Stop the mixer, scrape the bowl, and continue mixing on low speed. Slowly add the flour mixture and mix for about 2 minutes or until well combined, then add the chocolate chunk mixture and mix until just combined.
7. Using a cookie scoop, drop the scoops of dough on the cookie sheets about 2 inches apart.
8. Bake for 10–12 minutes.
9. Allow the cookies to cool on the baking sheets for 5 minutes, then transfer them to a wire rack to cool completely.

PRO TIP: For extra-toasty s'more cookies, use a kitchen torch to toast the marshmallows after baking.

Red Velvet Cookies

Makes: About 40 cookies | Prep Time: 30–40 minutes | Bake Time: 12–14 minutes

If you love red velvet cake, you might love these cookies even more! The ingredients that make red velvet cake delicious (buttermilk and vinegar) somehow magically produce a cookie that is perfectly crispy on the outside and chewy on the inside.

INGREDIENTS:

- **3 cups (450 g) all-purpose flour**
- **3 Tbsp (25 g) cocoa powder, sifted**
- **1 tsp baking soda**
- **¾ tsp salt**
- **1 Tbsp buttermilk***
- **2 eggs**
- **1½ tsp vanilla extract**
- **10 drops red gel food colouring**
- **1 cup (225 g) butter**
- **1½ cups (300 g) granulated sugar**
- **2 tsp vinegar**
- **½ cup (100 g) coarse sugar**

1. Position a rack in the centre of your oven and preheat it to 350°F. Line cookie sheets with parchment paper.
2. In a medium-sized bowl, add the flour, cocoa powder, baking soda, and salt. Whisk to combine and set aside.
3. In a glass measuring cup, add the buttermilk, eggs, vanilla, and food colouring. Combine with a wisk and set aside.
4. In the bowl of a stand mixer fitted with a paddle attachment, beat the butter on medium speed for about a minute. Gradually add the sugar. Stop the mixer, scrape the sides of the bowl with a spatula, and continue mixing on medium-high speed for 5–8 minutes or until the mixture becomes pale and fluffy.
5. Reduce the mixer speed to low and slowly pour in the buttermilk mixture. Mix for 30 seconds. Add the vinegar and continue mixing for another 30 seconds. Stop the mixer, scrape the bowl, then mix on medium-high speed for about a minute or until everything is well combined.
6. Stop the mixer, scrape the bowl, and switch to low speed. Gradually add the flour mixture and mix until everything is well combined and a smooth dough forms.
7. In a small bowl, add the coarse sugar. Using a cookie scoop, drop scoops of dough one by one into the bowl of coarse sugar. Use your fingers to roll the dough around the bowl to ensure they are evenly coated. Then place the coated cookie dough balls on the prepared cookie sheets about 2 inches apart.
8. Bake for 12–14 minutes.
9. Allow the cookies to cool on the baking sheets for 5 minutes, then transfer them to a wire rack to cool completely.

* *If you do not have buttermilk on hand, make your own by adding ¼ tsp of lemon juice or vinegar to a small bowl, then add 1 Tbsp of regular milk. Let stand for 5 minutes, stir, then use as you would regular buttermilk. It will not be quite the same as real buttermilk, but it can be used in a pinch!*

Valentine Cookies

Makes: About 40 cookies | Prep Time: 1½–2 hours (includes dough refrigeration)
Bake Time: 6–10 minutes

Originally a family tradition created by our mom, she would bake, decorate and beautifully arrange cookies on heart shaped plates for us to share with our classmates every Valentine's Day. Today, it is a permanent fixture on Crave's Valentine's Day menu, delighting customers each year.

RECIPES REQUIRED:

Vanilla Buttercream Frosting (pg 56)

INGREDIENTS:

- **2 cups (300 g) all-purpose flour**
- **½ tsp baking powder**
- **½ tsp baking soda**
- **½ tsp salt**
- **½ cup (113 g) butter**
- **½ cup (100 g) granulated sugar**
- **1 egg**
- **1 tsp vanilla extract**
- **2 Tbsp milk**

1. In a medium-sized bowl, add the flour, baking powder, baking soda, and salt. Whisk to combine and set aside.
2. In the bowl of a stand mixer fitted with a paddle attachment, beat the butter on medium speed for about a minute. Gradually add the sugar. Stop the mixer and use a spatula to scrape the sides of the bowl. Continue mixing on medium-high speed for 5–8 minutes or until the mixture becomes pale and fluffy.
3. Crack the egg into a small bowl. Turn the mixer to low and add the egg and then the vanilla. Stop the mixer and scrape the mixing bowl, then turn it to medium-high speed and mix for about a minute or until everything is well combined.
4. Stop the mixer, scrape the bowl, and continue to mix on low speed. Slowly add about half the flour mixture, then add the milk, and then add the remaining flour mixture. Continue to mix for 2 minutes or until a smooth dough forms.
5. Remove dough from the mixer and divide it into two even balls. Place each on a separate piece of plastic wrap and shape into flat discs. Wrap tightly and chill for at least an hour.
6. Position a rack in the centre of your oven and preheat it to 350°F. Line cookie sheets with parchment paper.
7. Place a well-chilled disc of dough on a floured work surface and sprinkle the top of the dough with flour. Position your rolling pin in the centre of the dough. Gently roll outward from the centre to the edge, applying even, gentle pressure as you work your way around the dough to create a circle-like shape. After every few rolls, lift and turn the dough to ensure it is not sticking to the surface. Sprinkle a little extra flour over and under the dough as needed. Roll until the dough is about ⅛ inch thick. >>

8. Use your desired cookie cutter to cut into shapes. Using an offset spatula, transfer the cookies to your prepared cookie sheets, placing them about 1 inch apart. Roll out scraps, and repeat once.
9. Bake for 6–10 minutes or until the bottoms are light golden brown.
10. Allow the cookies to cool on the baking sheet for 5 minutes, then transfer them to a wire rack to cool completely.
11. While the cookies are cooling, prepare the vanilla buttercream frosting, then use an offset spatula to spread buttercream frosting on top of the cookies.

Auntie Louise's Gingerbread Cookies

Makes: About 40 2-inch cookies | PrepTime: 1 ½ – 2 hours (includes dough refrigeration) | Bake Time: 6–10 minutes

This recipe comes from our Auntie Louise, who is a wonderful baker. We can remember her rolling these gingerbread cookies paper thin, placing them in the freezer, and then baking them into perfectly crispy cookies. We use this recipe to make our gingerbread people sandwich cookies for the Christmas holidays; however, a gingerbread cookie this good can be made any time of the year.

RECIPES REQUIRED:

Farmer's Butter Glaze (pg 40)

INGREDIENTS:

- **½ cup (100 g) granulated sugar**
- **¼ cup (67 g) water**
- **¼ cup (80 g) dark corn syrup**
- **2 tsp ginger**
- **1 tsp cinnamon**
- **2 tsp cloves**
- **½ cup (113 g) butter, softened and cut into 1-inch cubes**
- **2¼ cups (335 g) all-purpose flour**
- **¾ tsp baking soda**

1. Add the sugar, water, corn syrup, and spices into a medium-sized pot and bring to boil over medium-high heat, stirring constantly with a heatproof spatula or wooden spoon.
2. Remove the pot from the heat and add the cubed butter into the mixture. Using a spatula, thoroughly combine the butter into the sugar mixture.
3. Transfer the mixture into a medium-sized bowl and allow it to come to room temperature.
4. In the bowl of a mixer fitted with a paddle attachment, add the flour and baking soda. Turn the mixer on low to combine the ingredients.
5. Slowly add the cooled sugar mixture to the flour mixture. Mix on low until a smooth dough forms.
6. Remove the dough from the mixer and divide it into two even balls. Place each on a separate piece of plastic wrap and shape them into flat discs. Wrap tightly and chill for at least an hour.
7. Position a rack in the centre of your oven and preheat it to 350°F. Line cookie sheets with parchment paper.

>>

8 Place a well-chilled disc of dough on a floured work surface and sprinkle the top of the dough with flour. Position your rolling pin in the centre of the dough, and gently roll outward from the centre to the edge, applying even, gentle pressure as you work your way around the dough to create a circle-like shape. After every few rolls, lift and turn the dough to ensure it is not sticking to the surface. Sprinkle a little extra flour over and under the dough as needed. Roll until the dough is about ⅛ inch thick.

9 Use your desired cookie cutter to cut the dough into shapes. Using an offset spatula, transfer the cookies to your prepared cookie sheets, placing them about 1 inch apart. Roll out scraps, and repeat once.

10 Bake for 6–10 minutes or until golden brown.

11 Allow the cookies to cool on the baking sheet for 5 minutes, then transfer them to a wire rack to cool completely.

12 While the cookies are cooling, prepare the glaze. Once cooled, dip the tops of the cookies into the glaze and place them on a rack until it sets.

Pecan Sandwich Cookies

Makes: About 40 cookies | Prep Time: 1½–2 hours (includes dough refrigeration) | Bake Time: 7–10 minutes

This cookie is a delicious twist on our traditional Valentine's dough; it's enriched with brown sugar and pecans to add depth of flavour and a nutty crunch. Sandwiched with toffee pecan buttercream, it is truly delicious.

RECIPES REQUIRED:

Toffee Pecan Buttercream Frosting (pg 69)

INGREDIENTS:

- **1 cup (125 g) raw pecans**
- **2 ⅔ cups (400 g) all-purpose flour**
- **1 tsp baking powder**
- **1 tsp baking soda**
- **1 tsp salt**
- **1 cup (225 g) butter**
- **1 cup (200 g) brown sugar**
- **2 eggs**
- **2 tsp vanilla extract**

1 Place raw pecans in a food processor and pulse until the nuts are crumbly and start to stick to the side of the bowl.

2 In a large-sized bowl, add the ground pecans, flour, baking powder, baking soda, and salt. Whisk to combine and set aside.

3 In the bowl of a stand mixer fitted with a paddle attachment, beat the butter on medium speed for about a minute. Gradually add the brown sugar. Stop the mixer and scrape the sides of the bowl with a spatula. Continue mixing on medium-high speed for 5–8 minutes or until the mixture becomes pale and fluffy.

4 Crack the eggs into a small bowl. Stop the mixer and scrape the bowl. Turn it to low speed and add the eggs one by one, then add the vanilla. Turn the mixer to medium-high speed and mix for about a minute or until everything is well combined.

5 Stop the mixer, scrape the bowl, and continue to mix on low speed. Slowly add the flour mixture and mix for about a minute or until well combined.

6 Remove the dough from the mixer and divide it into two even balls. Place each on a separate piece of plastic wrap and shape them into flat discs. Wrap tightly and chill for at least an hour.

7 Position a rack in the centre of your oven and preheat it to 350°F. Line cookie sheets with parchment paper. >>

8 Place a well-chilled disc of dough on a floured work surface and sprinkle the top of the dough with flour. Position your rolling pin in the centre of the dough, and gently roll outward from the centre to the edge, applying even, gentle pressure as you work your way around the dough to create a circle-like shape. After every few rolls, lift and turn the dough to ensure it is not sticking to the surface. Sprinkle a little extra flour over and under the dough as needed. Roll until the dough is about ⅛ inch thick.

9 Use your desired cookie cutter to cut into shapes. Using an offset spatula, transfer the cookies to your prepared cookie sheets, placing them about 1 inch apart.

10 Bake for 7–10 minutes or until golden brown.

11 Allow the cookies to cool on the baking sheet for 5 minutes, then transfer them to a wire rack to cool completely.

12 While the cookies are cooling, prepare the toffee pecan buttercream. Follow the instructions on How to Pipe Buttercream Frosting onto Cupcakes (pg 16), but use a round tip to pipe buttercream onto the cookies.

Vanilla Thumbprint Cookies with Milk Chocolate Ganache (or Raspberry Jam)

Makes: About 40 cookies | Prep Time: 30 minutes | Bake Time: 18–22 minutes | Decorating Time: 20–30 minutes

This classic cookie is a favourite in our bakeries, where they are filled with milk chocolate ganache for the Christmas season. They are, however, equally delicious filled with raspberry jam, dark chocolate ganache, or caramel filling.

RECIPES REQUIRED:

Milk Chocolate Ganache (pg 42)

INGREDIENTS:

- **1 cup (225 g) butter**
- **¼ cup (50 g) granulated sugar**
- **1 tsp vanilla extract**
- **2 cups (300 g) all-purpose flour**

1 Position a rack in the centre of your oven and preheat it to 300°F. Line cookie sheets with parchment paper.

2 In the bowl of a stand mixer fitted with a paddle attachment, beat the butter on medium speed for about a minute. Gradually add the sugar. Stop the mixer and scrape the sides of the bowl with a spatula. Continue mixing on medium-high speed for 5–8 minutes or until the mixture becomes pale and fluffy.

3 Stop the mixer, scrape the bowl, and continue to mix on low speed. Add the vanilla, let it combine, then slowly add the flour. Mix for about 2 minutes or until the ingredients are well combined and a smooth dough forms.

4 Using a 1-inch cookie scoop or a teaspoon, scoop the cookie dough into your hands and roll it into balls. Place them on the prepared cookie sheets about 1 inch apart. Make an indentation in the middle of the cookies with your thumb or the back of a teaspoon.

5 Bake for 18–22 minutes or until the bottoms are light golden brown.

6 Let the cookies cool for 5 minutes, then press each indentation once more.

7 Transfer the cookies to a wire rack to cool completely.

>>

8 While the cookies are cooling, prepare the Milk Chocolate Ganache (pg 42).

9 Using a pastry bag or a spoon, fill the indentations with ganache. Allow the chocolate to set before storing.

Variations

Fill the thumbprint cookies with Dark Chocolate Ganache (pg 43), Raspberry Jam (pg 44), or Caramel Filling (pg 50).

Grandpa Starling's Shortbread Cookies

Makes: About 30 1½-inch cookies | Prep Time: 30 minutes | Bake Time: 15–18 minutes

This cherished recipe is actually Grandma Starling's, though we always made it as a Christmas treat for Grandpa Starling. Now a customer favourite during the holiday season in our bakeries, we've adapted the recipe for use with a stand mixer. However, feel free to embrace tradition and use your hands instead—just like we were taught by Grandma.

INGREDIENTS:

- **2 cups minus 2 Tbsp (265 g) all-purpose flour**
- **2 Tbsp cornstarch**
- **1 cup (225 g) butter, softened**
- **½ cup (65 g) icing sugar**

1. Position a rack in the centre of your oven and preheat it to 300°F. Line cookie sheets with parchment paper.
2. In a medium-sized bowl, add the flour and cornstarch. Whisk to combine and set aside.
3. In the bowl of a stand mixer fitted with a paddle attachment, beat the butter on medium speed for about a minute. Gradually add the icing sugar. Stop the mixer and scrape the sides of the bowl with a spatula. Continue mixing on medium-high speed for 5–8 minutes or until the mixture becomes pale and fluffy.
4. Stop the mixer, scrape the bowl, and continue to mix on low speed. Slowly add the flour mixture; mix for 2 minutes or until well combined and a smooth dough forms.
5. Place your dough on a lightly floured work surface and sprinkle the top with flour. Position your rolling pin in the centre of the dough, and gently roll outward from the centre to the edge, applying even, gentle pressure as you work your way around the dough to create a circle-like shape. Roll until the dough is about ½ inch thick.
6. Use a 1 ½ inch round or scallop cookie cutter to cut out cookies. Then, using an off-set spatula, transfer the cookies onto the prepared cookie sheet about 1 inch apart. Using a fork, mark the top of the cookies twice.
7. Bake for 15–18 minutes or until the bottom of the cookies are light golden brown.
8. Allow the cookies to cool on the baking sheet for 5 minutes, then transfer them to a wire rack to cool completely.

Twix Bar

Makes: One 8- × 8-inch square pan | Prep Time: 1½–2 hours | Bake Time: 15–18 minutes

This bar combines a classic shortbread crust, caramel filling, and a chocolate ganache topping. It began as a Christmas-only menu item, but our customers requested that we add it to the menu year-round. Once you make this bar, you'll understand why it's so popular.

RECIPES REQUIRED:

Milk Chocolate Ganache (pg 42)

INGREDIENTS:

Shortbread Crust

- **¾ cup (170 g) butter, softened**
- **½ cup (100 g) granulated sugar**
- **1¼ cups (185 g) all-purpose flour**

Caramel Filling

- **¾ cup (170 g) butter, softened and cut into 1-inch cubes**
- **¾ cup (150 g) brown sugar**
- **¾ cup (230 g) sweetened condensed milk**
- **3 Tbsp (60 g) dark corn syrup**
- **⅛ tsp flaky sea salt**

1. Position a rack in the centre of your oven and preheat it to 350°F. Butter an 8- × 8-inch square cake pan and line it with parchment paper trimmed to fit the bottom and the sides of the pan.
2. In the bowl of a stand mixer fitted with a paddle attachment, beat the butter on medium speed for about a minute. Gradually add the sugar. Stop the mixer and scrape the sides of the bowl with a spatula. Continue mixing on medium speed for 5–8 minutes or until the mixture becomes pale and fluffy.
3. Stop the mixer, scrape the bowl, and slowly add the flour. Continue to mix on low speed until everything is thoroughly combined and a smooth dough forms.
4. Remove the dough from the bowl and press it evenly into the prepared pan. Bake for 15–18 minutes, or until the top is light golden brown.
5. Place the pan on a wire rack to cool completely. While the crust is cooling in the pan, prepare the caramel filling.
6. In a medium-sized saucepan, melt the butter over medium heat. Then add the brown sugar, condensed milk, and dark corn syrup. Continue heating over medium-high heat and bring the mixture to a rolling boil, stirring continuously. Reduce the heat and boil for 4–5 minutes, still stirring.
7. Remove the saucepan from the heat and pour the caramel over the cooled shortbread crust. Sprinkle the salt evenly over the caramel and allow it to cool for 30 minutes.
8. While the filling is cooling, prepare the Milk Chocolate Ganache (pg 42). Pour ¾ cup of ganache over the bar, ensuring to completely cover the caramel filling.
9. Once the ganache has set, remove the bar from the pan and cut into 16 equal pieces.

Salted Nut Bar

Makes: One 8- × 8-inch square pan | Prep Time: 1½–2 hours | Bake Time: 35 minutes (crust + caramel)

Our bakeries have made this bar almost every Christmas since we started. Once, we decided to change things up and replaced it with a different bar. It became clear, very quickly, that our customers missed the salted nut bar in their holiday baking boxes, so it has faithfully returned every December since.

INGREDIENTS:

Shortbread Crust

- **¾ cup (170 g) butter, softened**
- **½ cup (100 g) granulated sugar**
- **1¼ cups (185 g) all-purpose flour**
- **1¾ cups (260 g) salted mixed nuts**

Caramel

- **⅓ cup (70 g) whipping cream**
- **⅓ cup (75 g) butter, softened and cut into 1-inch cubes**
- **¼ cup (80 g) dark corn syrup**
- **½ cup (130 g) granulated sugar**
- **⅓ cup (80 g) water**
- **2 tsp light corn syrup**

1 Position a rack in the centre of your oven and preheat it to 350°F. Butter an 8- × 8-inch square cake pan and line it with parchment paper trimmed to fit the bottom and the sides of the pan.

2 In the bowl of a stand mixer fitted with a paddle attachment, beat the butter on medium speed for about a minute. Gradually add the sugar. Stop the mixer and scrape the sides of the bowl with a spatula. Continue mixing on medium speed for 5–8 minutes or until the mixture becomes pale and fluffy.

3 Stop the mixer, scrape the bowl, and slowly add the flour. Continue to mix on low speed until everything is thoroughly combined and a smooth dough forms.

4 Remove the dough from the bowl and press it evenly into the prepared pan. Bake for 15–18 minutes, or until the top is light golden brown.

5 Place the pan on a wire rack to cool for 5 minutes, then sprinkle the nuts evenly over the crust.

6 While the crust is cooling in the pan, prepare the caramel. Keep the oven on.

7 In a glass measuring cup, combine the whipping cream, butter, and dark corn syrup. Microwave the mixture in 30-second increments until the cream begins to boil. Cover and set aside.

8 In a medium-sized saucepan, add the sugar, water, and light corn syrup and stir until combined.

9 Place a plate over top of the saucepan and bring the mixture to a boil over medium-high heat.

>>

10 Once the sugar mixture starts boiling, remove the plate and continue cooking, occasionally swirling the pan. Cook until the sugar mixture turns a golden amber colour around the edges.

11 Slowly pour the warm cream into the hot sugar, whisking constantly until combined. *Be sure to wear an oven mitt on your stirring hand, as there will be lots of steam, and the caramel will bubble and spatter.*

12 Return the saucepan to the stovetop on medium-high heat and clip a candy thermometer onto the side of the pan. Continue to cook the caramel, stirring occasionally, until the temperature reaches 235°F.

13 Slowly and evenly pour the caramel over the nuts. Bake for 12–15 minutes or until the caramel bubbles through to the centre.

14 Place the pan on a wire rack to cool completely, then remove the bar from the pan and cut into 16 pieces.

Triple Chocolate Brownie

Makes: One 8- × 8-inch square pan | Prep Time: 1½ hours | Bake Time: 45–60 minutes

Elevating a classic family dessert, this brownie is for chocolate lovers. Featuring three layers of chocolate, each with its own delightful texture, it's a bar worth eating every time. Fun fact, this bar is a Crave team member favourite!

RECIPE REQUIRED:
Dark Chocolate Ganache (pg 43)

INGREDIENTS:

Brownie Base

- **½ cup (75 g) all-purpose flour**
- **2 tsp cocoa powder, sifted**
- **¼ tsp salt**
- **⅔ cup (125 g) good quality dark chocolate chunks**
- **⅓ cup (75 g) butter**
- **½ cup (100 g) granulated sugar**
- **2 Tbsp brown sugar**
- **1 egg + 1 egg yolk**
- **1 tsp vanilla extract**

Chocolate Cream

- **1 cup (200 g) good quality dark chocolate chunks**
- **3 egg yolks**
- **¼ cup (50 g) granulated sugar**
- **⅔ cup (120 g) whipping cream**
- **⅔ cup (150 g) milk**

1 Position a rack in the centre of your oven and preheat it to 350°F. Butter an 8- × 8-inch square cake pan and line it with parchment paper trimmed to fit the bottom and the sides of the pan.

2 In a small bowl, add the flour, cocoa powder, and salt. Combine with a whisk and set aside.

3 In a medium-sized glass bowl, add the dark chocolate and butter. Microwave in 30-second increments, stirring with a spatula after each interval. Repeat this process until the butter and chocolate are melted.

4 Add the sugars into the melted chocolate mixture and whisk to combine. Then add the egg, egg yolk, and vanilla and whisk until smooth.

5 Using a spatula, gently fold the flour mixture into the chocolate mixture, just until combined.

6 Transfer the batter into the prepared pan and use an offset spatula or the back of a spoon to evenly spread it to the edges of the pan.

7 Bake for 18–22 minutes or until a toothpick inserted into the centre of the brownie comes out with a few moist crumbs.

8 Place the pan on a wire rack to cool completely. While the base is cooling, prepare the chocolate cream layer. Keep the oven on.

9 In a medium-sized bowl, add the chocolate chunks and set aside.

10 In a large-sized glass bowl, add the egg yolks and sugar. Vigorously whisk together for 2–3 minutes or until the mixture is thick and pale.

11 In a medium-sized saucepan, add the whipping cream and milk and bring to a boil. >>

12 Slowly pour two-thirds of the boiling cream mixture into the sugar mixture, whisking continuously.

13 Transfer the mixture back to the saucepan and whisk to combine. Continue to heat for 2–3 minutes or until the mixture has thickened and coats the back of a spoon.

14 Pour the mixture over the chocolate chunks and allow it to stand for 30 seconds. Vigorously mix with a whisk until all the chocolate has melted and the mixture is smooth.

15 Place a fine-mesh strainer over a medium-sized bowl and pour the mixture through the strainer. Transfer the mixture onto the cooled brownie base. Return the pan to the oven and bake for 25–30 minutes, or until the cream has set around the edges but is still jiggly in the centre.

16 Place the pan on a wire rack and let stand for 5 minutes, then cover with plastic wrap and allow it to cool completely.

17 While the cream layer is cooling, prepare the Dark Chocolate Ganache (pg 43). After the bar has cooled, pour ¾ cup of dark chocolate ganache over the bar, ensuring to completely cover the chocolate cream.

18 Once the ganache has set, remove the bar from the pan and cut into 16 equal pieces.

Magic Cookie Bar

Makes: One 8- × 8-inch square pan | Prep Time: 15–20 minutes | Bake Time: 30–35 minutes

Made with a buttery, crunchy cornflake base and layered with chocolate, coconut, and pecans, this bar is generously drizzled with sweetened condensed milk, resulting in a perfect and irresistible dessert.

INGREDIENTS:

- **4 cups (100 g) cornflakes, crushed**
- **¼ cup (55 g) granulated sugar**
- **½ cup (113 g) butter, melted**
- **1 cup (200 g) dark chocolate chunks**
- **1½ cups (150 g) shredded sweetened coconut**
- **1 cup (140 g) pecan pieces**
- **1 can (380 g) sweetened condensed milk**

1. Position a rack in the centre of your oven and preheat it to 350°F. Butter an 8- × 8-inch square cake pan and line it with parchment paper trimmed to fit the bottom and the sides of the pan.
2. In a medium-sized bowl, crush the cornflakes using your hands or a wooden spoon. Add the sugar and melted butter and mix until well combined.
3. Transfer the mixture into the prepared pan and use an offset spatula or the back of a spoon to evenly spread it to the edges of the pan.
4. Sprinkle the dark chocolate chunks evenly over the cornflake base, followed by the coconut and then the pecans.
5. Pour the can of condensed milk evenly over the layered ingredients, ensuring it reaches into the corners of the pan.
6. Bake for 30–35 minutes or until the top is golden brown.
7. Place the pan on a wire rack to cool completely, then remove the bar from the pan and cut into 16 equal pieces.

Date Bar

Makes: One 8- × 8-inch square pan | Prep Time: 20–30 minutes | Bake Time: 25–30 minutes

If you love dates, this bar will be your new favourite. Dates are nature's candy, and this bar offers a rich, caramel-like sweetness that is not only delicious but is also a wholesome and nourishing treat.

INGREDIENTS:

Oatmeal Crumble

- **1¼ cups (185 g) all-purpose flour**
- **1½ cups (150 g) large-flake oatmeal**
- **¾ cup (150 g) brown sugar**
- **½ tsp baking powder**
- **⅛ tsp baking soda**
- **¾ cup (170 g) butter, softened and cut into 1-inch cubes**

Date Filling

- **3 cups (425 g) dates**
- **1 cup (250 g) water**
- **2 Tbsp lemon juice**
- **1 Tbsp brown sugar**
- **½ tsp baking soda**

1 Position a rack in the centre of your oven and preheat it to 350°F. Butter an 8- × 8-inch square cake pan and line it with parchment paper trimmed to fit the bottom and the sides of the pan.

2 In the bowl of a stand mixer fitted with the paddle attachment, add the flour, oatmeal, brown sugar, baking powder, and baking soda. Turn the mixer to low speed and combine the ingredients.

3 Gradually add the cubed butter. Continue to mix until all the butter is combined and the mixture forms a crumble-like consistency. Transfer the mixture to a bowl and set it aside.

4 In a medium-sized saucepan, add the dates, water, lemon juice, and brown sugar. Place the saucepan on a stovetop over medium-high heat.

5 Bring the mixture to a boil and continue boiling until the dates soften and absorb all the liquid. Remove the saucepan from the heat, and using a spatula, stir the baking soda into the mixture.

6 To assemble the bar, transfer two-thirds of the crumble mixture into the prepared pan. Press the crumble evenly into the pan using your hands. Transfer the date mixture into the pan and use an offset spatula or the back of a spoon to spread it evenly to the edges of the pan. Top the dates evenly with the remaining crumble mixture and lightly press it down with your hands.

7 Bake for 25–30 minutes or until the top is golden brown.

8 Place the pan on a wire rack to cool completely, then remove the bar from the pan and cut into 16 pieces.

Pies

Our mom is an excellent pie maker, as was our grandmother before her, and their delicious pies were always a highlight at large family gatherings—a tradition we continue with our own families. We often have three to four different pies to ensure that everyone gets a slice of their favourite. At Crave, we honour the seasons with our pie offerings; summertime brings an array of pies made with in-season fruits, while Thanksgiving transforms our bakeries with the scent of freshly baked pumpkin pies.

The Ultimate Pie Pastry

Makes: 2 pie shells | Prep Time: 20–30 minutes

The following pastry recipe took over fifty iterations to perfect. It's based on our grandmother's original recipe, which was made entirely with lard. We wanted to enhance both the flavour and the pale colour that using lard produced, while maintaining the recipe's perfectly flaky texture. Through extensive testing of various ratios of lard, butter, and shortening, we found a greater proportion of lard to butter yields the best result. Lard ensures the crust's perfect flakiness, while the butter adds a rich flavour and colour.

INGREDIENTS:

- **¾ cup (170 g) cold lard, cut into 1-inch pieces**
- **¼ cup (55 g) cold butter, cut into 1-inch pieces**
- **⅓ cup (80 g) cold water**
- **1 Tbsp granulated sugar**
- **¾ tsp salt**
- **2½ cups (375 g) all-purpose flour**

1. Place the cubed lard and butter in a bowl and set in the freezer for at least 10 minutes, or until needed.
2. In a glass measuring cup, add the cold water, sugar, and salt. Using a fork, mix until the sugar and salt completely dissolve. Set the mixture in the freezer until needed.
3. In the bowl of a food processor fitted with the blade attachment, add the flour, half of the lard, and half of the butter, and pulse until blended. Then add the remaining lard and butter and continue to pulse until the mixture has a coarse, cornmeal-like consistency.
4. Turn the food processor on and add the water mixture in one steady stream through the opening. Turn the processor off once all the water is absorbed and a dough begins to form.
5. Flour your work surface, then remove the pastry from the food processor and gently knead the rough bits of dough and any remaining flour until combined. Divide the dough into two even balls, place each on a separate piece of plastic wrap, and shape into flat discs. Wrap them tightly and chill for at least 1 hour.

PRO TIP: Using a food processor speeds up the process. However, if you do not have one, use a pastry blender to incorporate the ingredients together.

A Few Pastry

How-Tos

How to Roll Perfectly *Flaky* Pastry

- Place your well-chilled disc of dough on a floured work surface and sprinkle the top of the pastry with flour. Start with your rolling pin at the centre of the dough, and gently roll outward from the centre to the edge, applying even, gentle pressure. Work your way around the dough to form a circle-like shape. After every few rolls, lift and rotate the dough to ensure it is not sticking to the surface. Sprinkle a little extra flour over and under the pastry as needed. Continue rolling until the dough is about ⅛ inch thick.

PRO TIP: Every time we make pastry, we remember our grandmother's advice: "Handle the dough lightly; do not overwork it—gentle, gentle." Keep this in mind and you will make perfectly flaky pastry every time.

How to *Line* a Pie Plate with Pastry (Single-Crust Pie)

- After rolling out the pastry (pg 166), place your pie plate on the pastry and use a small paring knife to cut a circle about 1½ inches larger than the plate's edge.
- Fold the pastry in half, then gently place it in the centre of your pie plate. Unfold the pastry and fit it to the bottom of the plate by lifting the edge of the pastry and gently pushing it into the bottom of the pan. Use your fingers and follow the bottom edge of the pie plate to ensure there are no gaps between the pastry and the pie plate.
- Gently fold the pastry hanging over the pie plate under so it is lined up with the edge of the plate. Pinch the pastry together to form a smooth edge. Then, using both of your hands, crimp the pastry between your fingers.

How to *Blind Bake* a Pie Crust

Blind baking a pie crust means baking a crust before adding a filling, and is required for custard style pie. This method is used to make Chocolate Banana Cream Pie (pg 183) and Coconut Cream Pie (pg 185).

- **You will need half a recipe (one disc) of the Ultimate Pie Pastry (pg 161)**

- Position a rack in the centre of your oven and preheat it to 375°F.
- After lining your pie plate with pastry (pg 167), cover it with a tea towel or plastic wrap and refrigerate for 30 minutes. Remove from the refrigerator and use a fork to evenly prick the pie pastry bottom and sides. Then line the pastry with tinfoil, ensuring the top crust of the pie is fully covered.
- Pour in 2 cups of dry white beans or uncooked rice (or whatever you have on hand to act as weight) and bake for 20–25 minutes. Remove the foil and weights and return to the oven for 5–10 minutes, or until the crust is golden brown.
- Proceed with the recipe as directed.

How to Make a *Double*-Crust Pie

- **You will need one full recipe (two discs) of the Ultimate Pie Pastry (pg 161).**

- To prepare the bottom crust, refer to the instructions for How to Line a Pie Plate with Pastry (pg 167), but leave the pastry hanging over the edge of the pan.
- Fill the pie according to the recipe, and cover with a tea towel or plastic wrap while you roll another disc of dough for the top of the pie.

Full TOP:

- Roll the second disc of dough, following the instructions for How to Roll Perfectly Flaky Pastry (pg 166). Cut holes (air vents) into the pastry using small cookie cutters, or keep it classic and simply use a knife to make 8–10 one-inch cuts. Fold the pastry in half and place it on the centre of the pie, then gently unfold it and centre it over the filling. Fold the pastry that is hanging over the pie plate under, along with the pastry from the bottom crust, and pinch the two together to create a seal. Then, using both of your hands, crimp the pastry between your fingers. Next, use a pastry brush to brush the top of the pie with whipping cream, then sprinkle with granulated sugar. Bake according to the recipe.

Lattice TOP:

- Roll the second disc of dough following the instructions for How to Roll Perfectly Flaky Pastry (pg 166). Using a pastry wheel (or pizza cutter), cut the pastry into strips of dough about 1 inch wide. Start the lattice by placing the longest strip over the middle of the pie, and continue covering the top of the pie with half of the strips, setting them about ¼ inch apart. Turn the pie 90 degrees and fold back every other strip until they are almost off the pie. Place your first strip on top, then unfold the strips back over the strips you just placed down. Then fold the other strips back, place a strip on top, then unfold the strips back again. Repeat this process until the pie is covered. Trim off any excess strips of pastry so they are the same length as the bottom crust. Fold the pastry hanging over the pie plate under, along with the pastry from the bottom crust, and pinch the two together to create a seal. Then, using both of your hands, crimp the pastry between your fingers. Use a pastry brush to brush the top of the pie with whipping cream, then sprinkle with granulated sugar. Bake according to the recipe.

How To *Line* a Cupcake Tin with Pastry

- **For making mini pies or tarts in a cupcake tin, you will need half a recipe (one disc) of the Ultimate Pie Pastry (pg 161).**

- After rolling out the pastry (pg 166), use a 4-inch cookie cutter to cut 12 circles of pastry.
- Place the circles of pastry into the cupcake tin, ensuring the pastry fits into the bottom of the pan (it is okay if it ruffles along the edges).
- Fill the pastry with the filling until it is almost to the top. Bake according to the recipe.

Raspberry Sour Cream Pie

Makes: One 9-inch pie | Prep Time: 20 minutes | Bake Time: 45–50 minutes

This is one of our all-time favourite pie recipes; it was kindly shared with us by one of our dearest former employees, Aldene Atkinson. The versatile custard mixture can be paired with any type of fruit, but raspberries are our favourite.

RECIPES TO PREPARE BEFORE YOU BEGIN:

1 batch of the Ultimate Pie Pastry (pg 161)

1 batch of Brown Sugar Crumb Topping (pg 39)

INGREDIENTS:

- **¾ cup (75 g) pecan pieces, untoasted**
- **1 cup (200 g) granulated sugar**
- **⅓ cup (50 g) all-purpose flour**
- **1¼ cups (320 g) sour cream**
- **2 eggs**
- **1 tsp vanilla extract**
- **1¼ cups (340 g) fresh raspberries**

1. Position a rack in the centre of your oven and preheat it to 400°F. Prepare a single pie crust, referring to the instructions for How to Line a Pie Plate with Pastry (pg 167).
2. In a medium-sized bowl, combine 1½ cups (260 g) of the prepared brown sugar crumbs with the pecan pieces and set aside.
3. In a large-sized bowl, whisk together the sugar and flour. Add the sour cream, eggs, and vanilla, then vigorously whisk the mixture until it is smooth.
4. Using a spatula, gently fold the raspberries into the sour cream mixture until they are evenly distributed.
5. Transfer the filling into the prepared pastry-lined pie plate.
6. Evenly sprinkle the brown sugar crumb mixture over the filling.
7. Bake at 400°F for 15 minutes. Then reduce the oven temperature to 325°F and bake for an additional 30–40 minutes.
8. Place the pie on a wire rack and allow it to cool completely (4–5 hours) before serving. Note: This pie is best served slightly chilled.

Strawberry Rhubarb Pie

Makes: One 9-inch pie / Prep Time: 20 minutes / Bake Time: 55–65 minutes

This pie embodies the essence of summer in a dessert; with rhubarb abundant and paired with strawberries, the combination of sweet and tangy flavours is sure to be a hit at BBQs and picnics.

RECIPES TO PREPARE BEFORE YOU BEGIN:
The Ultimate Pie Pastry (pg 161)

INGREDIENTS:
- **¾ cup (150 g) brown sugar**
- **½ cups (75 g) all-purpose flour**
- **1¼ cup (340 g) chopped strawberries, fresh or frozen**
- **1 cup (300 g) chopped rhubarb (1-inch pieces), fresh or frozen**

1 Position a rack in the centre of your oven and preheat it to 400°F. Prepare the bottom pie crust, referring to the instructions for How to Line a Pie Plate with Pastry (pg 167).

2 In a large-sized bowl, combine the brown sugar and flour with a spatula. Add the fruit and gently mix until the pieces are evenly coated. Then transfer the coated fruit into the prepared pastry-lined pie plate.

3 Top the fruit with the pastry, choosing a method from the instructions for How to Make a Double-Crust Pie (pg 169).

4 Bake at 400°F for 15 minutes. Then reduce the oven temperature to 350°F and continue baking for an additional 30–40 minutes.

5 Place the pie on a wire rack and allow it to cool completely (4–5 hours) before serving.

PRO TIP: If using frozen fruit, you may need to increase the baking time.

Variation:

This pie is also delicious topped with Brown Sugar Crumb Topping (pg 39) instead of pastry.

Pumpkin Pie

Makes: One 9-inch pie | Prep Time: 20 minutes | Bake Time: 45–60 minutes for a large pie

During Thanksgiving, you will find our bakeries smelling of delicious pumpkin pies. We make both large and mini pies, and we top them with Cream Cheese Buttercream Frosting. It's hard to say which is people's favourite—large or mini—so we'll give you the recipes for both and you can make your own decision.

RECIPES TO PREPARE BEFORE YOU BEGIN:

The Ultimate Pie Pastry (pg 161)

RECIPES REQUIRED:

Cream Cheese Buttercream Frosting (pg 61)

INGREDIENTS:

- **1½ cups (200 g) pumpkin purée**
- **1 cup (200 g) brown sugar**
- **1 cup (185 g) evaporated milk**
- **1 tsp cinnamon**
- **½ tsp nutmeg**
- **¼ tsp ginger**
- **¼ tsp salt**
- **2 eggs**

1. Position a rack in the centre of your oven and preheat it to 400°F. Prepare a a single pie crust, referring to How to Line a Pie Plate with Pastry (pg 167).
2. In a large-sized bowl, add the pumpkin purée, brown sugar, milk, spices, and salt. Vigorously whisk the mixture until smooth. Allow it to rest for at least 10 minutes to absorb the spices.
3. Add the eggs to the mixture and whisk until well combined.
4. Pour the filling into the prepared pastry-lined pie plate.
5. Bake in the oven at 400°F for 15 minutes, then reduce the temperature to 325°F and bake for an additional 30–40 minutes.
6. Remove the pie from the oven and place it on a wire rack to cool completely before serving.
7. While the pie is cooling, prepare the Cream Cheese Buttercream Frosting (pg 61), then pipe dollops onto the top of the pie.

NOTE: It can be difficult to know when a pumpkin pie has finished baking. For a perfectly baked pie, insert a knife 1 inch from the middle of the pie. If it comes out clean, it is done. If a few crumbs remain on the knife, bake for another 2–3 minutes.

Variation:

MINI PIES (OR TARTS): Follow the instructions for How to Line a Cupcake Tin with Pastry (pg 172). Then continue with the recipe as stated above. Using a cookie scoop or a spoon, fill the pastry-lined cupcake tin with the pumpkin filling almost to the top. Bake for 30–35 minutes.

Butter Tarts

Makes: 12 tarts / Prep Time: 20–25 minutes / Bake Time: 25–30 minutes

This was our dad's favourite Christmas treat, and he claimed our mom made the best butter tarts in the country. Although he has not been with us for a long time, we think of him every year as our bakeries produce this quintessential holiday treat. The following recipe is the one our mom made; however, in our bakeries we use half currants and half golden raisins, skipping the walnuts and coconut. Feel free to make this your own and choose what you would like to add.

RECIPES TO PREPARE BEFORE YOU BEGIN:

The Ultimate Pie Pastry (pg 161)

INGREDIENTS:

- **⅓ cup (75 g) butter**
- **¾ cup (150 g) brown sugar**
- **2 eggs**
- **1 tsp vanilla extract**
- **¾ cup currants, washed and drained**
- **¼ cup chopped walnuts (optional)**
- **¼ cup shredded sweetened coconut (optional)**

1. Position a rack in the centre of your oven and preheat it to 350°F.
2. Line a cupcake tin with pastry, referring to How to Line a Cupcake Tin with Pastry (pg 172).
3. In the bowl of a stand mixer fitted with a paddle attachment, beat the butter on medium speed for about a minute. Gradually add the brown sugar. Stop the mixer and use a spatula to scrape the sides of the bowl. Continue mixing on medium-high speed for 10–12 minutes or until the mixture becomes pale and fluffy (this takes a long time!).
4. Crack the eggs into a small bowl. Turn the mixer to low and add the eggs one by one. Stop the mixer and scrape the sides of the mixing bowl. Add the vanilla, then turn the mixer to medium-high speed and mix for about a minute or until everything is well combined.
5. Remove the bowl from the mixer and gently fold in the currants, walnuts, and coconut.
6. Using a small cookie scoop or a spoon, scoop the filling into the prepared pastry-lined cupcake pan.
7. Bake for 25–30 minutes or until the pastry is golden brown.
8. Remove the pan from the oven and allow the tarts to cool for 15 minutes. Then, using an offset spatula, gently remove the tarts from the cupcake pan, transfer them to a wire rack, and allow them to cool completely before serving.

Chocolate Banana Cream Pie

Makes: One 9-inch pie | Prep Time: 20–30 minutes | Bake Time: 30–35 minutes

This has always been a family favourite, from the time we were children. Now we love to make it for our own families.

RECIPES TO PREPARE BEFORE YOU BEGIN:
The Ultimate Pie Pastry (pg 161)

RECIPES REQUIRED:
Chocolate Custard (pg 48)

INGREDIENTS:

- **1 cup (240 g) whipping cream**
- **¼ cup (35 g) icing sugar**
- **1 tsp vanilla extract**
- **3 bananas, sliced ¼-inch thick**

1. Prepare a blind-baked crust, referring to How to Blind Bake a Pie Crust (pg 168).
2. Allow the crust to cool completely before assembling the pie.
3. Prepare one batch of Chocolate Custard (pg 48). Pour the freshly made custard into the cooled pie crust. Using an offset spatula, or the back of a spoon, smooth the custard to the edges of the pie shell. Place a piece of plastic wrap directly on the surface of the custard to prevent a skin from forming. Allow the custard to cool for at least 60 minutes.
4. Just before serving, prepare your whipped cream and sliced bananas. Start by placing the whipping cream in a large bowl.
5. Using a hand-held mixer, whip the cream on the highest setting until it starts to thicken.
6. Stop the mixer, add the icing sugar, turn the mixer to medium speed, and mix until all the icing sugar has been absorbed. Stop the mixer and add the vanilla.
7. Turn the mixer to the highest speed and continue to mix for 3–4 minutes or until medium peaks form.
8. Evenly arrange the banana slices over the chocolate custard.
9. Dollop whipped cream on top of the bananas. Using an offset spatula, gently spread the whipped cream to cover the bananas.

PRO TIP: Whipped cream is best when made just before serving. To expedite the process, keep the beaters and bowl cooling in the fridge prior to whipping the cream.

Coconut Cream Pie

Makes: One 9-inch pie | Prep Time: 1 ½ hours | Bake Time: 10–15 minutes

Irresistibly tropical, coconut cream pie is a dessert that's sure to please. Whether enjoyed as a comforting treat on a cozy evening or at a celebratory gathering, this pie stands as a timeless symbol of decadence.

RECIPES TO PREPARE BEFORE YOU BEGIN:

Graham Cracker Crumbs, fine (pg 36)

RECIPES REQUIRED:

Coconut Custard (pg 47)

INGREDIENTS:

- **¾ cup (75 g) shredded sweetened coconut**
- **2 cups (260 g) graham cracker crumbs, finely ground**
- **¼ cup (50 g) granulated sugar**
- **¼ cup (55 g) butter, melted**
- **1 cup (240 g) whipping cream**
- **¼ cup (35 g) icing sugar**
- **1 tsp vanilla extract**

1. Position a rack in the centre of your oven and preheat it to 350°F. Line a cookie sheet with parchment paper.
2. Sprinkle the coconut onto the prepared cookie sheet. Bake for 5 minutes. The outer edges of the coconut will toast faster, so stir it with a spatula to combine the toasted coconut with the untoasted coconut. Bake for another 3 minutes, then stir again. Repeat this process until the coconut is evenly golden brown. Allow it to cool for at least 5 minutes before using.
3. In a large-sized bowl, combine ¼ cup of the cooled toasted coconut with the graham cracker crumbs and sugar. Using a spatula, add the melted butter and mix until all the ingredients are thoroughly combined.
4. Transfer the graham crumb mixture into a pie plate. Using your hands, press the crumbs evenly into the bottom and sides of the pie plate.
5. Bake for 10–15 minutes or until the crust is golden brown. Place it on a wire rack and allow it to cool for at least 30 minutes.
6. Prepare one batch of Coconut Custard (pg 47). Pour the freshly made custard into the cooled pie crust. Using an offset spatula, or the back of a spoon, smooth the custard to the edges of the pie shell. Place a piece of plastic wrap directly on the surface of the custard to prevent a skin from forming. Allow the custard to cool for at least 60 minutes.
7. Just before serving, prepare your whipped cream. Start by placing the whipping cream in a large bowl.
8. Using a hand-held mixer, whip the cream on the highest setting until it starts to thicken.

>>

9 Stop the mixer, add the icing sugar, turn the mixer to medium speed, and mix until all the icing sugar has been absorbed. Stop the mixer and add the vanilla.

10 Turn the mixer to the highest speed and continue to mix for 3–4 minutes or until medium peaks form.

11 Dollop whipped cream on top of the coconut custard. Using an offset spatula, or the back of a spoon, gently spread the whipped cream to cover the custard. Sprinkle the remaining toasted coconut on top of the whipped cream.

PRO TIP: Whipped cream is best when made just before serving. To expedite the process, keep the beaters and bowl cooling in the fridge prior to whipping the cream.

Add white sugar when this has boiled (Stir) Change sp Wipe with

1/3 c. marg.
Fold in: 3/4 c. currants (washed + drained)
walnuts
coconut
8 - 10 min.

Date

From the kitchen of: Granma
Recipe for: Ginger Snaps
Ingredients:
Sift together — 3 cups
1/2 tsp s
2 tsp b. soda
1/2 tsp cloves
1 tsp ginger
1 tsp cinnamon
Cream well 3/4 cup marg
1 cup b. sugar
Artwork from Wood River Gallery, Mill Valley, California

Carrot – Pineapple Muffins
1 1/2 c all purpose flour
1 c sugar
1 tsp baking soda (1 tsp b. p)
1 tsp salt, 1 tsp cin
2/3 c oil
2 eggs

shortening
b. sugar
c. w. sugar
egg
c. vanilla

Whipped Shortbread
1 c butter
1/2 c icing sugar
1/2 c cornstarch
1 1/2 c flour
1/4 tsp salt
Beat butter until fluffy, add icing sugar while beating. Blend in cornstarch. Add flour & salt. Drop by tsp on cookie sheet. Bake at 375 ... until light brown. 2 dozen

Butter Squares.
12 ozs. butterscotch chips
3/4 cup peanut butter.
1/2 cup butter.
Melt over hot water. (Not the burner).
Add 1 small pkg. of marsh mallows. Above must be cool

Cream Pie:
cup raisins + 3/4 c water — until
sour cream.
sugar.
flour.

Soak
Add
Dry Mix - 1 cup
1 1/2 tsp. B.
1/2 tsp soda
3/4 cup. b. sug
Pour wet into dry - MIX Lightly
Fold in 1 cup blue berries.

Eagle Brand Dessert
1 can eagle b
1 32 oz.

1/2 c.
2/3 c.
1/2 c.
1/2 c.
1 t.
Comb in water.
until boils.
boil 5 min.
Stir in butt

To Mom
2 cups whole unb
1/2 cup sugar
2 tablespoons unsalted
1/2 teaspoons vanilla
3/4 teaspoon salt
In a 9-inch fryin heat almonds sugar and butter over medium heat stirring constantly until golden brown, about 15 minutes. Remove from heat and stir in vanilla. Spread mixture on lightly battered foil or a baking sheet. Sprinkle with salt. Cool completely and break into clusters. Makes about 2.
Love Your Daughter
Jodi McIntyre

From the kitchen of: Grandma
Recipe for: Apple Pie
Ingredients:
- 3/4 cup of sugar
- dot with butter (small pieces)
- Sprinkle with cinnamon
425° 10 mins
350° 25 mins
Brush pastry lightly with cream - to make brown.
Artwork from Wood River Gallery, Mill Valley, California

Rhubarb
1/2 c. mar
1 1/2 c. su
1 egg

noms) 370° - in new oven - 375° - 35 mins
2 tbs. swansdown
sugar
egg whites
salt
c. of tartar
ugar

Lemon Pork
4 chops (floured
Place in
4 lemon
Sauce

IF BEING A ... WERE EAS... A DAD COULD DO IT!
with spoon
while now
at medium
boil
butter

Mom's Old, Old Ch
2 sq. semi-sweet ch
2/3 c. milk
1 1/2 c. sugar
dash salt
2T butter
1t. vanilla
1c. walnuts

From the kitchen of: Grandma S + Mom
Recipe for: Pumpkin Pie
Ingredients:
2 eggs slightly beat (3 eggs, if doubled)
pumpkin
(scant)

Loaves

Loaves are a classic homemade staple and are quick and easy to make. We love having them on hand for breakfast, a quick snack for lunches, or a simple dessert. In the following section you'll find a few of our favourite recipes. They are very versatile and swapping out ingredients is encouraged. Orange or grapefruit can be used in place of lemon in the Lemon Poppyseed Loaf, while strawberries or any fresh fruit in season can work in the Raspberry Crumb Loaf.

Lemon Poppyseed Loaf

Makes: One 8- × 5-inch loaf | Prep Time: 15–25 minutes | Bake Time: 60–70 minutes

An old-time classic, this loaf brings together the bright, zesty flavour of lemon with the delicate crunch of poppy seeds. It's then topped with a tangy lemon glaze.

INGREDIENTS:

- **1¾ cups (260 g) all-purpose flour**
- **2 tsp baking powder**
- **½ tsp salt**
- **1 cup (200 g) granulated sugar**
- **3 eggs**
- **⅓ cup (85 g) canola oil**
- **1 cup (260 g) sour cream**
- **2 Tbsp poppy seeds (omit if you want plain lemon loaf)**
- **2 Tbsp (60 g) lemon juice, freshly squeezed**
- **2 Tbsp lemon zest**
- **½ tsp vanilla extract**
- **2 tbsp (60g) freshly squeezed lemon juice**
- **½ cup (65 g) icing sugar**

1. Position a rack in the centre of your oven and preheat it to 350°F. Butter an 8- × 5-inch loaf pan and line it with parchment paper.
2. In a medium-sized bowl, add the flour, baking powder, and salt. Combine with a whisk and set aside.
3. In a large-sized bowl, add the sugar, eggs, and oil. Vigorously mix with a whisk for 1–2 minutes or until the mixture is pale in colour. Add the sour cream, poppy seeds, 2 Tbsp of lemon juice, lemon zest, and vanilla. Mix with a whisk until combined.
4. Using a spatula, gently fold the flour mixture into the sugar mixture until just combined.
5. Transfer the batter into the prepared loaf pan. Bake for 60–70 minutes or until a probe thermometer inserted into the centre of the loaf reads 200°F.
6. Allow the loaf to cool in the pan for 10 minutes, then remove it from the pan and transfer it to a wire rack to cool completely before glazing.
7. While the loaf is cooling, prepare the glaze by mixing the icing sugar and 2 Tbsp of lemon juice in a medium-sized bowl until it is smooth.
8. Using a silicone pastry brush, brush the top and sides of the loaf with the glaze. Allow the glaze to set before serving.

Banana Chocolate Loaf

Makes: One 8- × 5-inch loaf | Prep Time: 15–25 minutes | Bake Time: 60–70 minutes

We have tested many banana bread recipes, and we think we have finally perfected it. The secret lies in using equal amounts of butter and oil. Butter contributes a rich flavour, while the oil guarantees a moist crumb. If you prefer, feel free to use either all butter or all oil. The addition of chocolate chunks is completely optional; Carolyne likes no chocolate, Jodi likes chocolate!

INGREDIENTS:

- **1¾ cups (260 g) all-purpose flour**
- **1 tsp baking powder**
- **1 tsp baking soda**
- **¼ tsp salt**
- **4 very ripe bananas**
- **1 cup (200 g) firmly packed brown sugar**
- **⅓ cup (75g) butter, melted**
- **⅓ cup (85g) canola oil**
- **⅓ cup (80g) milk**
- **2 eggs**
- **2 tsp vanilla extract**
- **½ cup (100 g) dark chocolate chunks (optional)**

1. Position a rack in the centre of your oven and preheat it to 350°F. Butter an 8- × 5-inch loaf pan and line it with parchment paper.
2. In a medium-sized bowl, add the flour, baking powder, baking soda, and salt. Combine with a whisk and set aside.
3. Place bananas in a large bowl and mash well with the back of a fork. Then add the sugar, melted butter, oil, milk, eggs, and vanilla. Vigorously mix with a whisk for 1–2 minutes or until well combined.
4. Using a spatula, gently fold the flour mixture into the banana mixture until just combined. Then fold in the chocolate chunks, if using.
5. Transfer the batter into the prepared loaf pan. Bake for 60–70 minutes or until a probe thermometer inserted into the centre of the loaf reads 200°F.
6. Allow the loaf to cool in the pan for 10 minutes, then remove it from the pan and transfer it to a wire rack to cool completely.

Marble Loaf

Makes: One 8- × 5-inch loaf | Prep Time: 15–25 minutes | Bake Time: 60–70 minutes

This is the loaf for those who love chocolate and vanilla equally—because it has both!

RECIPES REQUIRED:

½ batch of Farmer's Butter Glaze (pg 40)

INGREDIENTS:

- **2 cups (300 g) all-purpose flour**
- **¾ tsp baking powder**
- **¾ tsp salt**
- **1½ cups (300 g) granulated sugar**
- **⅓ cup (85 g) canola oil**
- **¼ cup (55 g) butter, melted**
- **⅔ cup (170 g) sour cream**
- **3 eggs**
- **1 egg yolk**
- **1 Tbsp vanilla extract**
- **3 Tbsp (25 g) cocoa powder, sifted**

1 Position a rack in the centre of your oven and preheat it to 350°F. Butter an 8- × 5-inch loaf pan and line it with parchment paper.

2 In a medium-sized bowl, add the flour, baking powder, and salt. Combine with a whisk and set aside.

3 In a large-sized bowl, add the sugar, oil, and melted butter, vigorously whisk together for a minute. Then add the sour cream, eggs, egg yolk, and vanilla, and vigorously whisk for 1–2 minutes or until the mixture is pale in colour.

4 Using a spatula, gently fold the flour mixture into the sugar mixture until combined.

5 Transfer half of the batter into a medium-sized bowl. Gently fold the cocoa powder into one of the bowls of batter and mix until combined.

6 To assemble the loaf, alternate adding layers of vanilla and chocolate batter into the prepared pan, adding about half a cup of batter each time. Spread each layer evenly with an offset spatula or the back of a spoon until it reaches the edges of the pan. Repeat twice.

7 Once the batter is layered into the pan, use an offset spatula or knife to swirl through the batter a few times to create a marbled effect.

8 Bake for 60–70 minutes or until a probe thermometer inserted into the centre of the loaf reads 200°F.

9 Allow the loaf to cool in the pan for 10 minutes, then remove it from the pan and transfer it to a wire rack to cool completely before glazing. While the loaf is cooling, prepare half a batch of the Farmer's Butter Glaze (pg 40).

10 Using a silicone pastry brush, glaze the top and sides of the loaf with the glaze. Half a recipe should be enough to glaze the loaf approximately twice.

Raspberry Crumb Loaf

Makes: One 8- × 5-inch loaf | Prep Time: 25–30 minutes | Bake Time: 60–70 minutes

The versatility of this loaf makes it perfect for breakfast, brunch, dessert, or anytime in between. Whether served at a weekend brunch or tucked into a lunchbox for a midday treat, it's sure to brighten any day.

RECIPES TO PREPARE BEFORE YOU BEGIN:

Brown Sugar Crumb Topping (pg 39)

INGREDIENTS:

- **1¼ cups (185 g) all-purpose flour**
- **½ tsp baking powder**
- **½ tsp salt**
- **⅔ cup (170 g) sour cream**
- **½ tsp vanilla extract**
- **¾ cup (170 g) butter**
- **1 cup (200 g) granulated sugar**
- **2 eggs**
- **1 egg yolk**
- **¾ cup (150 g) raspberries, fresh or frozen**
- **¾ cup (150 g) brown sugar crumb topping**

1. Position a rack in the centre of your oven and preheat it to 350°F. Butter an 8 × 5-inch loaf pan and line it with parchment paper.
2. In a medium-sized bowl, add the flour, baking powder, and salt. Combine with a whisk and set aside.
3. In a glass measuring cup, add the sour cream and vanilla.
4. In the bowl of a stand mixer fitted with a paddle attachment, beat the butter on medium speed for about a minute. Gradually add the sugar. Stop the mixer and scrape the sides of the bowl with a spatula. Continue mixing on medium speed for 5–8 minutes or until the mixture becomes pale and fluffy.
5. Crack the eggs and egg yolk into a small bowl. Turn the mixer to low and add the eggs one by one. Stop the mixer and scrape the mixing bowl, then turn the mixer to medium-high speed and mix for about a minute or until everything is well combined.
6. Reduce the mixer speed to low and add half of the flour mixture, then add the sour cream and vanilla mixture. Mix for 30 seconds, then add the remaining flour and continue mixing for 30 seconds to combine. Stop the mixer, scrape the bowl, then mix on medium-high for a minute or until everything is well combined.
7. Remove the bowl from the mixer and using a spatula gently fold the raspberries into the batter.
8. Transfer the batter into the prepared loaf pan. Top with the brown sugar crumbs. Bake for 60–70 minutes or until a probe thermometer inserted into the centre of the loaf reads 200°F.
9. Allow the loaf to cool in the pan for 10 minutes, then remove it from the pan and transfer it to a wire rack to cool completely.

Zucchini Pecan Loaf

Makes: One 8- × 5-inch loaf / Prep Time: 25–30 minutes / Bake Time: 60–70 minutes

This delicious zucchini loaf is the perfect way to use up the abundance of fresh zucchini in the fall.

RECIPES REQUIRED:

½ batch of Farmer's Butter Glaze (pg 40)

INGREDIENTS:

- **½ cup (50 g) pecan pieces, toasted**
- **1¾ cups (265 g) all-purpose flour**
- **2 tsp cinnamon**
- **1 tsp baking soda**
- **½ tsp salt**
- **Pinch baking powder**
- **1 ⅓ cups (265 g) granulated sugar**
- **½ cup (120 g) canola oil**
- **2 eggs**
- **2 tsp vanilla extract**
- **2 cups (200 g) zucchini, grated with peel left on**

1. Position a rack in the centre of your oven and preheat it to 350°F. Butter an 8- × 5-inch loaf pan and line it with parchment paper.
2. Place the pecan pieces on a cookie sheet lined with parchment paper and toast them in the oven for 5–8 minutes. Allow them cool for at least 10 minutes.
3. In a medium-sized bowl, add the flour, cinnamon, baking soda, salt, and baking powder. Combine with a whisk and set aside.
4. In a large-sized bowl, add the sugar, oil, and eggs. Vigorously mix with a whisk for 1–2 minutes or until the mixture is pale in colour, then mix in the vanilla and zucchini.
5. Using a spatula, gently fold the flour mixture into the sugar mixture, and mix until just combined. Then add the toasted pecan pieces.
6. Transfer the batter into the prepared loaf pan. Bake for 60–70 minutes or until a probe thermometer inserted into the centre of the loaf reads 200°F.
7. Allow the loaf to cool in the pan for 10 minutes, then remove it from the pan and transfer it to a wire rack to cool completely before glazing. While the loaf is cooling, prepare half a batch of the Farmer's Butter Glaze (pg 40).
8. Using a silicone pastry brush, brush the top and sides of the loaf with the glaze. Half a recipe should be enough to glaze the loaf approximately twice.

Gluten-Free & Vegan Cupcakes, Cakes, & Cookies

Although we are not a certified gluten-free or vegan bakery, the demand for allergy-friendly options inspired us to create a selection of gluten-free and vegan cupcakes and cookies. Perfecting these products was a process; our goal was to match the taste of our original products as closely as possible. It took us some time, but we are excited to share our recipes, complete with our simple substitutions. In our bakeries, we use Cup4Cup flour, but feel free to use your favourite gluten-free blend.

Gluten-Free Chocolate Cake with Vava Vanilla Buttercream Frosting

Makes: Two 8-inch cakes | Prep Time: 20 minutes | Bake Time: 25–30 minutes
Decorating Time: 10–30 minutes

This is the original chocolate cake that inspired us to start Crave, adapted to be gluten-free. We spent many hours of recipe testing to make the gluten free version taste as good as our original—and we think we accomplished it. We've even had customers call it "holy whack amazing." We hope you feel the same way.

RECIPES REQUIRED:

Vava Vanilla Buttercream Frosting (pg 57)

INGREDIENTS:

- **1 cup (250 g) milk**
- **½ cup (120 g) canola oil**
- **2 eggs**
- **2 tsp vanilla extract**
- **3 cups (450 g) gluten-free flour**
- **2¾ cups (550 g) granulated sugar**
- **½ cup (60 g) cocoa powder, sifted**
- **1 tsp baking powder**
- **1 tsp baking soda**
- **¾ tsp salt**
- **1 cup (250 g) boiling water**

1. Position a rack in the centre of your oven and preheat it to 350°F. Butter two 8-inch round cake pans and place parchment paper at the bottom of each pan.
2. Begin boiling water by turning on your kettle.
3. In a small bowl, add the milk, oil, eggs, and vanilla. Whisk to combine and set aside.
4. In the bowl of a stand mixer fitted with a paddle attachment, add the flour, sugar, cocoa powder, baking powder, baking soda, and salt. Turn mixer to low speed to combine the ingredients.
5. While the mixer is on low speed, slowly add the milk mixture. Mix for 30 seconds. Then, keeping the mixer on low speed, gradually pour in the boiling water. Mix for about 30 seconds. Stop the mixer, scrape the bowl, and then mix at medium speed for a minute or until well combined.
6. Transfer the batter into the prepared pans and bake for 25–30 minutes or until a toothpick inserted into the centre comes out clean.
7. Allow the cakes to cool for 10 minutes, then remove them from the pans and transfer them to a wire rack to cool completely before frosting.
8. While the cakes are cooling, prepare the Vava Vanilla Buttercream Frosting (pg 57), then refer to the instructions for How to Ice a Two-Layer Cake (pg 18).

>>

Variations

CUPCAKES: Line two cupcake tins with cupcake papers. Using a cookie scoop or a spoon, scoop the batter into the prepared pans, filling each well about two-thirds full. Bake for 18–23 minutes.

SHEET CAKE: Butter a 9- × 13-inch cake pan and place parchment paper at the bottom of the pan. Transfer the batter into the prepared pan and bake for 25–30 minutes.

Gluten-Free Red Velvet Cake with Cream Cheese Buttercream Frosting

Makes: Two 8-inch cakes | Prep Time: 20–30 minutes | Bake Time: 30–35 minutes
Decorating Time: 10–30 minutes

Inspired by customer requests to expand our gluten-free product line, we launched red velvet cupcakes topped with our signature Cream Cheese Buttercream Frosting. This delicious addition is a customer favourite.

RECIPES REQUIRED:

Cream Cheese Buttercream Frosting (pg 61)

INGREDIENTS:

- **1½ cups (400 g) buttermilk***
- **¾ cup (170 g) canola oil**
- **4 eggs**
- **1½ tsp vanilla extract**
- **10–15 drops red gel food colouring**
- **3½ cups (500 g) gluten-free flour**
- **2½ cups (500 g) granulated sugar**
- **3 Tbsp (25 g) cocoa powder, sifted**
- **1½ tsp baking soda**
- **1½ tsp salt**
- **½ tsp vinegar**

1. Position a rack in the centre of your oven and preheat it to 350°F. Butter two 8-inch round cake pans, and place parchment paper at the bottom of each pan.
2. In a medium-sized bowl, add the buttermilk, oil, eggs, vanilla, and gel food colouring. Combine with a whisk and set aside.
3. In the bowl of a stand mixer fitted with a paddle attachment, add the flour, sugar, cocoa powder, baking soda, and salt. Turn the mixer to low speed to combine the ingredients.
4. Slowly add the oil mixture to the flour mixture. Mix for 30 seconds. Add the vinegar and continue mixing for another 30 seconds. Stop the mixer, scrape down the sides of the bowl, then turn the mixer to medium-high speed and beat for 1 minute.
5. Transfer the batter into the prepared pans and bake for 30–35 minutes or until a toothpick inserted into the centre comes out clean.
6. Allow the cakes to cool for 10 minutes, then remove them from the pans and transfer them to a wire rack to cool completely before frosting.
7. While the cakes are cooling, prepare the Cream Cheese Buttercream Frosting (pg 61), and then refer to the instructions for How to Ice a Two-Layer Cake (pg 18).

>>

* *If you do not have buttermilk on hand, make your own by adding 1½ Tbsp of lemon juice or vinegar to a glass measuring cup, then fill with regular milk to make 1½ cups. Let stand for 5 minutes, stir, then use as you would regular buttermilk. It will not be quite the same as real buttermilk, but it can be used in a pinch!*

Variations

CUPCAKES: Line two cupcake tins with cupcake papers. Using a cookie scoop or a spoon, scoop the batter into the prepared pans, filling each well about two-thirds full. Bake for 25–30 minutes.

SHEET CAKE: Butter a 9- × 13-inch cake pan and place parchment paper at the bottom of the pan. Transfer the batter into the prepared pan and bake for 25–30 minutes.

Gluten-Free Vanilla Cupcakes with Chocolate Buttercream Frosting

Makes: 18–24 cupcakes / Prep Time: 15–20 minutes / Bake Time: 25–30 minutes
Decorating Time: 10–30 minutes

Crafting this cake was challenging, as the subtlety of vanilla means that every nuance in flavour is tasted. Through diligent testing, we've perfected the recipe. We are excited to say our entire cupcake menu is now available gluten-free.

RECIPES REQUIRED:

Chocolate Buttercream Frosting (pg 59)

INGREDIENTS:

- **1¾ cups (450 g) milk**
- **2 Tbsp canola oil**
- **1 Tbsp vanilla extract**
- **3 cups (450 g) gluten-free flour**
- **1¾ cups (350 g) granulated sugar**
- **1 Tbsp baking powder**
- **¾ tsp salt**
- **¾ cup (170 g) butter, softened and cut into 1-inch pieces**
- **3 eggs**

1. Position a rack in the centre of your oven and preheat it to 350°F. Line two cupcake tins with cupcake papers.
2. In a glass measuring cup, add the milk, oil, and vanilla. Whisk to combine and set aside.
3. In the bowl of a stand mixer fitted with a paddle attachment, add the flour, sugar, baking powder, and salt. Turn mixer to low speed to combine the ingredients.
4. Slowly add the cubed butter and continue mixing for 1–2 minutes until fully incorporated into the dry ingredients. Your mixture will have a crumbly texture.
5. Crack the eggs into a small bowl, turn the mixer to low, and add the eggs one by one. Mix for 30 seconds. Then slowly add the milk mixture. Mix for another 30 seconds.
6. Stop the mixer and scrape the mixing bowl, then turn the mixer to medium-high speed and mix for about a minute or until everything is well combined.
7. Using a cookie scoop or a spoon, scoop the batter into the prepared pans and bake for 25–30 minutes or until a toothpick inserted into the centres comes out clean.
8. Allow the cupcakes to cool for 10 minutes, then remove them from the pans and transfer them to a wire rack to cool completely before frosting.

>>

9 While the cupcakes are cooling, prepare the Chocolate Buttercream Frosting (pg 59), then refer to the instructions for How to Pipe Buttercream Frosting onto Cupcakes (pg 16).

Variations

LAYER CAKE: Butter two 8-inch round cake pans and place parchment paper at the bottom of each pan. Divide the batter equally among the two prepared pans. Bake the cakes for 30–35 minutes or until a toothpick inserted into the centres comes out clean.

SHEET CAKE: Butter a 9- × 13-inch cake pan and place parchment paper at the bottom of the pan. Transfer the batter into the prepared pan and bake for 25–30 minutes.

Gluten-Free Chocolate Chip Cookies

Makes: About 40 cookies | Prep Time: 20 minutes | Bake Time: 12–15 minutes

We have a passion for making the best chocolate chip cookies. We took that passion to heart when creating our gluten-free version, and in the taste test, most people could not tell the difference between the regular and gluten-free; it's that good!

INGREDIENTS:

- **2¾ cups (430 g) gluten-free flour**
- **1 tsp baking soda**
- **¾ tsp salt**
- **1 cup (225 g) butter**
- **1 cup (200 g) granulated sugar**
- **1 cup (200 g) firmly packed brown sugar**
- **2 eggs**
- **2 tsp vanilla extract**
- **1 cup (200 g) dark chocolate chips or chunks**
- **1 cup (200 g) chocolate, roughly chopped**
- **2 tsp flaky sea salt (optional)**

1. Position a rack in the centre of your oven and preheat it to 350°F. Line cookie sheets with parchment paper.
2. In a medium-sized bowl, add the flour, baking soda, and salt. Whisk to combine and set aside.
3. In the bowl of a stand mixer fitted with a paddle attachment, beat the butter on medium speed for about a minute. Gradually add the sugars. Stop the mixer and scrape the sides of the bowl with a spatula. Continue mixing on medium-high speed for 5–8 minutes or until the mixture becomes pale and fluffy.
4. Crack the eggs into a small bowl. Turn the mixer to low and add the eggs one by one, then add the vanilla. Mix for 30 seconds. Stop the mixer and scrape the mixing bowl, then turn the mixer to medium-high speed and mix for about a minute or until everything is well combined.
5. Stop the mixer, scrape the bowl, and continue mixing on low speed. Slowly add the flour mixture and mix for about 2 minutes or until well combined. Then add the chocolate chips and chopped chocolate and mix until just combined.
6. Using a cookie scoop, drop the cookie dough onto the prepared cookie sheets about 2 inches apart. If desired, sprinkle the top of each cookie with the flaky sea salt.
7. Bake for 12–15 minutes.
8. Allow the cookies to cool on the baking sheets for 5 minutes, then transfer them to a wire rack to cool completely.

Gluten-Free Confetti Cookies

Makes: About 40 cookies | Prep Time: 20 minutes | Bake Time: 12–15 minutes

We tested lots of different flour combinations for this recipe and landed on a half and half combo of gluten-free flour and almond flour. If you are allergic to nuts, replace the almond flour with gluten-free flour.

INGREDIENTS:

- **1¾ cups (280 g) gluten-free flour**
- **2 cups (220 g) almond flour**
- **1 tsp baking soda**
- **½ tsp baking powder**
- **½ tsp salt**
- **1 cup (225 g) butter**
- **1¾ cups (350 g) granulated sugar, plus another ½ cup (100 g) for coating the cookie dough**
- **2 eggs**
- **1 Tbsp vanilla extract**
- **⅓ cup (60 g) rainbow (or other) sprinkles**

1. Position a rack in the centre of your oven and preheat it to 350°F. Line cookie sheets with parchment paper.
2. In a medium-sized bowl, add the flours, baking soda, baking powder, and salt. Whisk to combine and set aside.
3. In the bowl of a stand mixer fitted with a paddle attachment, beat the butter on medium speed for about a minute. Gradually add the sugar. Stop the mixer and use a spatula to scrape the sides of the bowl. Continue mixing on medium speed for 5–8 minutes or until the mixture becomes pale and fluffy.
4. Crack the eggs into a small bowl. Turn the mixer to low and add the eggs one by one, then add the vanilla. Mix for 30 seconds. Stop the mixer and scrape the sides of the bowl, then turn the mixer to medium-high speed and mix for about a minute or until everything is well combined.
5. Stop the mixer, scrape the bowl, and continue to mix on low speed. Slowly add the flour mixture and mix for about 2 minutes or until well combined. Then add the sprinkles and mix until just combined.
6. In a small bowl, add the ½ cup of sugar. Using a cookie scoop, drop the scoops of dough one by one into the bowl of sugar. Use your fingers to roll the dough around the bowl to ensure it is evenly coated. Then place the coated cookie dough balls on the prepared cookie sheets about 2 inches apart.
7. Bake for 12–15 minutes.
8. Allow the cookies to cool on the baking sheets for 5 minutes, then transfer them to a wire rack to cool completely.

Vegan Chocolate Cake with Chocolate Frosting

Makes: Two 8-inch cakes | Prep Time: 20 minutes | Bake Time: 30–35 minutes
Decorating Time: 10–30 minutes

This is the original chocolate cake, the one that inspired us to start Crave, but with a twist: it's vegan. You simply remove the eggs from the original recipe and replace the volume with applesauce. We tried a few vegan egg substitutes, but we felt the applesauce gave the cake the best flavour, and honestly, you would not even know it's missing eggs!

RECIPES REQUIRED:
Vegan Chocolate Frosting (pg 223)

INGREDIENTS:

- **2½ cups (375 g) all-purpose flour**
- **2 cups (400 g) granulated sugar**
- **½ cup (60 g) cocoa powder, sifted**
- **2 tsp baking powder**
- **2 tsp baking soda**
- **¾ tsp salt**
- **⅔ cup (170 g) canola oil**
- **⅓ cup (100 g) applesauce**
- **2 tsp vanilla extract**
- **2 cups (500 g) boiling water**

1. Position a rack in the centre of your oven and preheat it to 350°F. Butter two 8-inch round cake pans with non-dairy butter and place parchment paper at the bottom of each pan.
2. Begin boiling water by turning on your kettle.
3. In the bowl of a stand mixer fitted with a paddle attachment, add the flour, sugar, cocoa powder, baking powder, baking soda, and salt. Turn mixer to low speed to combine the ingredients.
4. Stop the mixer and add the oil, applesauce, and vanilla. Mix for 30 seconds. Turn the mixer to low speed, pour in the boiling water, and mix for another 30 seconds. Stop the mixer, scrape the sides of the bowl, and mix at medium speed for 1½ minutes.
5. Transfer the batter into the prepared pans and bake for 30–35 minutes or until a toothpick inserted into the centre comes out clean.
6. Allow the cakes to cool for 10 minutes, then remove them from the pans and transfer them to a wire rack to cool completely before frosting.
7. While the cakes are cooling, prepare the Vegan Chocolate Frosting (pg 223), and then refer to the instructions for How to Ice a Two-Layer Cake (pg 18).

>>

Vegan Chocolate Cake with Vegan Chocolate Frosting (pg 221–23), Vegan Chocolate Cupcakes with Vegan Vanilla Frosting (pg 221, 225)

Variations

CUPCAKES: Line two cupcake tins with cupcake papers. Transfer the chocolate batter into a glass measuring cup (note it will not all fit at once), and pour it into the prepared pans, filling each well to the top. Bake for 14–18 minutes.

SHEET CAKE: Butter a 9- × 13-inch cake pan with non-dairy butter and place parchment paper at the bottom of the pan. Transfer the batter into the prepared pan and bake for 25–30 minutes.

Vegan Chocolate Frosting

Makes: About 5 cups | Prep Time: 10–15 minutes

We started our vegan (or non-dairy) line with chocolate frosting. We are proud to say, it tastes just as good as our original!

INGREDIENTS:

- **5 cups (650 g) icing sugar**
- **½ cup (60 g) cocoa powder, sifted**
- **⅓ cup (80 g) oat milk or other non-dairy milk**
- **1 Tbsp vanilla extract**
- **1 ⅓ cups (300 g) non-dairy butter**

1. Measure the icing sugar and cocoa powder into a small bowl. Whisk together and set it aside.
2. Measure the oat milk and vanilla into a glass measuring cup or small bowl and set aside.
3. In the bowl of a stand mixer fitted with a paddle attachment, beat the non-dairy butter on medium speed for a minute.
4. Stop the mixer and scrape the sides of the bowl. Turn the mixer to low speed and slowly add the icing sugar mixture. Mix until well combined, then slowly add the oat milk and vanilla. Continue to mix on low for about a minute.
5. Stop the mixer, scrape the bowl, then turn the mixer to medium-high speed and beat for 5–10 minutes or until it is light and fluffy.
6. Place any leftover frosting in an airtight container and store in the fridge for up to 5 days or in the freezer for up to 3 months.

NOTE: To determine when your frosting is ready, scoop a small amount of it onto your spatula, then gently tap it against the side of the bowl. If the frosting easily falls off the spatula, it is ready. If it stays on the spatula, continue mixing it on medium-high speed until it reaches the desired consistency.

Vegan Vanilla Frosting

Makes: About 5 cups | Prep Time: 10–15 minutes

Our classic Crave-o-licious cupcakes are the most popular baked good in our bakeries. After discovering Becel Plant Butter, we re-created our signature vanilla buttercream frosting to be dairy-free. With or without added colour, it tastes just as delicious as the original.

INGREDIENTS:

- **5 cups (650 g) icing sugar**
- **⅓ cup (80 g) oat milk or other non-dairy milk**
- **1 Tbsp vanilla extract**
- **1 ⅓ cups (300 g) non-dairy butter**
- **Food colouring (for variations)**

1. Measure the icing sugar into a small bowl and set it aside.
2. Measure the oat milk and vanilla into a glass measuring cup or small bowl and set aside.
3. In the bowl of a stand mixer fitted with a paddle attachment, beat the non-dairy butter on medium speed for about a minute.
4. Stop the mixer and scrape the sides of the bowl. Turn the mixer to low speed and slowly add the icing sugar. Mix until well combined, then slowly add the oat milk and vanilla. Continue to mix on low for about a minute.
5. Turn off the mixer, scrape down the sides of the bowl again, and add any desired food colouring. Then turn the mixer to medium-high speed and beat for 5–10 minutes or until it is light and fluffy.
6. Place any leftover frosting in an airtight container and store in the fridge for up to 5 days or in the freezer for up to 3 months.

NOTE: To determine when your frosting is ready, scoop a small amount of it onto your spatula, then knock it on the side of the bowl. If the frosting easily falls off the spatula, it is ready. If it stays on the spatula, continue to mix on medium-high speed until it reaches the desired consistency.

Variations

CRAVE-O-LICIOUS FROSTING: Add 3 drops of violet and 2 drops of royal blue gel food colouring.

VAVA VANILLA FROSTING: Add 3 drops of pink gel food colouring.

MINT FROSTING: Substitute peppermint extract for vanilla extract. Use 3 drops of leaf green gel food colouring.

Vegan Chocolate Chip Cookies

Makes: About 40 cookies | Prep Time: 20 minutes | Bake Time: 12–15 minutes

This is our original chocolate chip cookie recipe, but it is made with non-dairy butter and we substitute oat milk for eggs; feel free to use any non-dairy milk.

INGREDIENTS:

- **2¾ cups (405 g) all-purpose flour**
- **1 tsp baking soda**
- **1 tsp salt**
- **1 cup (225 g) non-dairy butter**
- **1 cup (200 g) granulated sugar**
- **1 cup (200 g) firmly packed brown sugar**
- **⅓ cup (80 g) oat milk or other non-dairy milk**
- **2 tsp vanilla extract**
- **1¾ cups (300 g) vegan dark chocolate chips**
- **2 tsp flaky sea salt (optional)**

1. Position a rack in the centre of your oven and preheat it to 350°F. Line cookie sheets with parchment paper.
2. In a medium-sized bowl, add the flour, baking soda, and salt. Whisk to combine and set aside.
3. In the bowl of a stand mixer fitted with a paddle attachment, beat the non-dairy butter on medium speed for about a minute. Gradually add the sugars. Stop the mixer and scrape the sides of the bowl with a spatula. Continue mixing on medium-high speed for 3–5 minutes or until the mixture becomes pale and fluffy.
4. Stop the mixer, scrape the mixing bowl, then add the oat milk and vanilla. Mix for 30 seconds. Then turn the mixer to medium-high speed and mix for about a minute or until everything is well combined.
5. Turn the mixer to low speed and slowly add the flour mixture. Mix for 2 minutes or until well combined. Add the chocolate chips and mix until just combined.
6. Using a cookie scoop, drop the cookie dough onto the prepared cookie sheets about 2 inches apart. If desired, sprinkle the top of each cookie with the flaky sea salt.
7. Bake for 12–15 minutes.
8. Allow the cookies to cool on the baking sheets for 5 minutes, then transfer them to a wire rack to cool completely.

Vegan Confetti Cookies

Makes: About 40 cookies | Prep Time: 10–12 minutes | Bake Time: 15–20 minutes

This is the bestselling vegan cookie in our bakeries. Add your favourite sprinkles to the dough and you will have a party in a cookie.

INGREDIENTS:

- **2¼ cups (335 g) all-purpose flour**
- **1 tsp baking soda**
- **1 tsp salt**
- **½ tsp baking powder**
- **1 cup (225 g) non-dairy butter**
- **1¾ cups (350 g) granulated sugar, plus another ½ cup (100 g) for coating the cookie dough**
- **⅓ cup (80 g) oat milk, or other non-dairy milk**
- **1 Tbsp vanilla extract**
- **⅓ cup (60 g) rainbow (or other) sprinkles**

1. Position a rack in the centre of your oven and preheat it to 350°F. Line cookie sheets with parchment paper.
2. In a medium-sized bowl, add the flour, baking soda, salt, and baking powder. Whisk to combine and set aside.
3. In the bowl of a stand mixer fitted with a paddle attachment, beat the non-dairy butter on medium speed for about a minute. Gradually add the sugar. Stop the mixer and scrape the sides of the bowl with a spatula. Continue mixing on medium speed for 3–5 minutes until the mixture becomes pale and fluffy.
4. Stop the mixer, scrape the sides of the bowl, and add the oat milk and vanilla. Mix for 30 seconds. Then turn to medium-high speed and mix for about a minute or until everything is well combined.
5. Turn the mixer to low speed and slowly add the flour mixture. Mix for 2 minutes or until well combined. Add the sprinkles and mix until just combined.
6. In a small bowl, add the ½ cup of sugar. Using a cookie scoop, drop the scoops of dough one by one into the bowl of sugar. Use your fingers to roll the dough around the bowl to ensure it is evenly coated. Then place the coated cookie dough balls on the prepared cookie sheets about 2 inches apart.
7. Bake for 10–12 minutes.
8. Allow the cookies to cool on the baking sheets for 5 minutes, then transfer them to a wire rack to cool completely.

Acknowledgements

We have so much gratitude towards all the individuals who contributed to making our dream of writing a cookbook a reality. The support and effort of all involved reflects the importance of collaboration and community in achieving goals. We are fortunate to be surrounded by so many lovely people. Thank you to our publisher Touchwood Editions. Nara and Tori, thank you for taking our project on. Your insight and encouragement was invaluable on our journey to writing our first cookbook.

We extend our heartfelt appreciation to our families for their unwavering support and boundless love. Your understanding during this time, as we took over the kitchens in our homes to create the delectable array of cookies, pies, and loaves for our photoshoot, means more to us than words can express. We are truly grateful for your presence, encouragement, and understanding throughout our journey.

We extend our deepest gratitude to our dedicated Crave team for their unwavering commitment to baking from scratch and sharing our passion for creating delicious treats. To all our teams who meticulously reviewed recipes and ensured flawless baking for our photo shoot, your dedication has been instrumental in bringing our vision to life.

A special thank-you goes out to Michelle, whose invaluable support during the photo shoots, from planning and styling to shopping and even lending a hand for those perfect shots, is truly appreciated.

We also express our heartfelt appreciation to our talented photographer, Genevieve, whose creativity, impeccable style, and endless patience transformed each picture into a work of art.

To Chantelle, your patience and humour while modelling for our cookbook photoshoot was terrific. Cendra, your product organization, test baking, and on-site cake decorating were extremely helpful. Thank you both for your dedication and hard work over the past ten years with Crave.

To our dear friends who have stood by us throughout the years, your support has meant the world to us. In particular, we extend our sincere thanks to Julie, Nadine, Lori, Izzy, Brenda, Alyssa, Lesley, and Antoinette for their invaluable feedback and suggestions, for going over recipes with us one more time, and for sharing your thoughtful insights.

To our cherished customers, we offer our heartfelt gratitude for your unwavering support and appreciation of the baking we craft each day. For the past two decades, you have walked through our doors, bringing our creations into your homes and sharing them with your loved ones. Your loyalty and enthusiasm have been the driving force behind Crave, reminding us daily of why we embarked on this journey. It is your smiles, your satisfaction, and your enjoyment of our baking that inspire us to continue pushing the boundaries of creativity and flavours. Thank you for being a part of our story and for making every moment of the past twenty years truly special.

Together you have all played a vital role in our journey, and we are profoundly grateful for your support, contributions, love, and friendship.

Index

T

U

V

W

Z

Conversion Chart

VOLUME

Imperial	Metric
⅛ tsp	0.5 mL
¼ tsp	1 mL
½ tsp	2.5 mL
¾ tsp	4 mL
1 tsp	5 mL
½ Tbsp	8 mL
1 Tbsp	15 mL
1½ Tbsp	23 mL
2 Tbsp	30 mL
2½ Tbsp	38 mL
¼ cup	60 mL
⅓ cup	80 mL
½ cup	125 mL
⅔ cup	165 mL
¾ cup	185 mL
1 cup	250 mL
1¼ cups	310 mL
1⅓ cups	330 mL
1½ cups	375 mL
1⅔ cups	415 mL
1¾ cups	435 mL
2 cups/ 1 pint	500 mL
2¼ cups	560 mL
2⅓ cups	580 mL
2½ cups	625 mL
2⅔ cups	665 mL
2¾ cups	690 mL
3 cups	750 mL
3½ cups	875 mL
4 cups	1 L
5 cups	1.25 L
6 cups	1.5 L
8 cups / 2 quarts	2 L
25 cups	6 L
25 cups	6 L

WEIGHT

Imperial	Metric
1 oz	30 g
4 oz	115 g
8 oz	225 g
10 oz	250 g
12 oz	340 g
1 lb (16 oz)	450 g
2 lb	900 g
5 lb	2,250 g

CANS

Imperial	Metric
6 oz	177mL
10 oz	284 mL
11oz	300ml
14 oz	398 mL
16 oz	480 mL
28 oz	796 mL

OVEN TEMPERATURE

Imperial	Metric
200°F	95°C
225°F	105°C
250°F	120°C
275°F	135°C
300°F	150°C
325°F	160°C
350°F	180°C
375°F	190°C
400°F	200°C
425°F	220°C
450°F	230°C

LENGTH/WIDTH

Imperial	Metric
1/12 inch	2 mm
⅛ inch	3 mm
⅙ inch	4 mm
¼ inch	6 mm
½ inch	12 mm
¾ inch	2 cm
1 inch	2.5 cm
1½ inches	3.5 cm
2 inches	5 cm
2½ inches	6.5 cm
3 inches	7.5 cm
3½ inches	9 cm
4 inches	10 cm
5 inches	12.5 cm
6 inches	15 cm
7 inches	18 cm
8 inches	20 cm
9 inches	23 cm
10 inches	25 cm

TEMPERATURE

(For oven temperatures, see chart below)

Imperial	Metric
115°F	46°C
150°F	66°C
160°F	71°C
170°F	77°C
180°F	82°C
185°F	85°C
190°F	88°C
200°F	93°C
240°F	116°C
247°F	119°C
250°F	121°C
290°F	143°C
300°F	149°C
350°F	177°C
360°F	182°C
370°F	188°C

US FLUID OUNCES

US fluid ounces	US customary	Metric
¼ oz	½ Tbsp / 1½ tsp	7.5 mL
⅓ oz	2 tsp	10 mL
½ oz	1 Tbsp	15 mL
¾ oz	1½ Tbsp / 4½ tsp	22 mL
1 oz (1 shot)	2 Tbsp	30 mL
1¼ oz	2½ Tbsp	37.5 mL
1½ oz	3 Tbsp	45 mL
2 oz	¼ cup	60 mL
2½ oz	5 Tbsp	75 mL
3 oz	¼ cup + 2 Tbsp	90 mL
3½ oz	¼ cup + 3 Tbsp	105 mL
4 oz	½ cup	125 mL
4½ oz	½ cup + 1 Tbsp	140 mL
5 oz	½ cup + 2 Tbsp	155 mL

Notes

TouchWood Editions
Touchwoodeditions.com

Edited by Christine Savage
Proofread by Marial Shea
Cover and interior design by Jazmin Welch

CATALOGUING DATA AVAILABLE FROM LIBRARY AND ARCHIVES CANADA
ISBN (print) 9781771514521
ISBN (electronic) 9781771514538

TouchWood Editions gratefully acknowledges that the land on which we live and work is within the traditional territories of the Lkwungen (Esquimalt and Songhees), Malahat, Pacheedaht, Scia'new, T'Sou-ke and W̱SÁNEĆ (Pauquachin, Tsartlip, Tsawout, Tseycum) peoples.

We acknowledge the financial support of the Government of Canada through the Canada Book Fund, and the province of British Columbia through the Book Publishing Tax Credit.

This book was produced using FSC®-certified, acid-free papers, processed chlorine free, and printed with soya-based inks.

Printed in China

28 27 26 25 2 3 4 5

From the kitchen of: Grandma
Recipe for: Pastry
Ingredients: - always tender flake lard (1 lb. roomtemp)
- cut into 8 ###
- 5½ cups loose packed flour
- small tbsp. salt (3/4)
- mix with "light" hands until all the lumps of lard are gone
- 1 cup of water into the middle of the mixture
- bring all the pastry into the middle
- wherever dry add the rest of the water
- mix lightly into the middle of the bowl

Artwork from Wood River Gallery, Mill Valley, California

RECIPES

Puffed Wheat
½c. butter
1c. b. sugar
2t. vanilla
½c. syrup
2t. cocoa
8c. puffed wheat
soft ball

Valentine
½c. shortening
½c. w. sugar
1 egg
2T. milk
1t. vanilla
2c. flour
½t. b powder
½t. b. soda
½t. salt
350° - lightly
cookie sheet

Brown-Eyed Susans
1c. marg
3T. sugar
1t. almond extract
2c. flour
Cream marg. Add sugar, extract and flour. Roll level T of mixture into balls. Greased cookie sheet - Flatten slightly - 400° - 10-12min.

Huckleberry Pie
chopped apples
rhubarb
raspberries
blueberries etc
½ - ¾ c sugar
¼ - ½ c of flour

Grandma Starling's Shortbread
flour
cut 2T flour
2T cornstarch
butter
2c. icing sugar - a little at a time
add flour mixture
fork
300°

Valentine Cookies
350° - lightly greased cookie sheet - 7-9min.

Cheese Crisps
Isobel McIntyre
2 cups rice crispies
2 " sharp cheddar cheese
2 " flour (3/4)
1 " marg (butter) ½ tsp salt
½ tsp. worcester sauce
Method: Beat butter & cheese (shredded) & cream well. Add flour gradually salt. Make ... Fold in crispies ... balls & flatten ...

Peanut Butter
Cream: 1c. p. bu...
1c. mar...
Add: 1c. w. sug...
1c. b sug...
2 eggs
1t. vanill...
2½c. flo...

A Recipe For: Scones.
Serves:
Preparation Time:
4 3/4 c. flour
1 T. b. powder
3/4 t. b. soda
... sugar